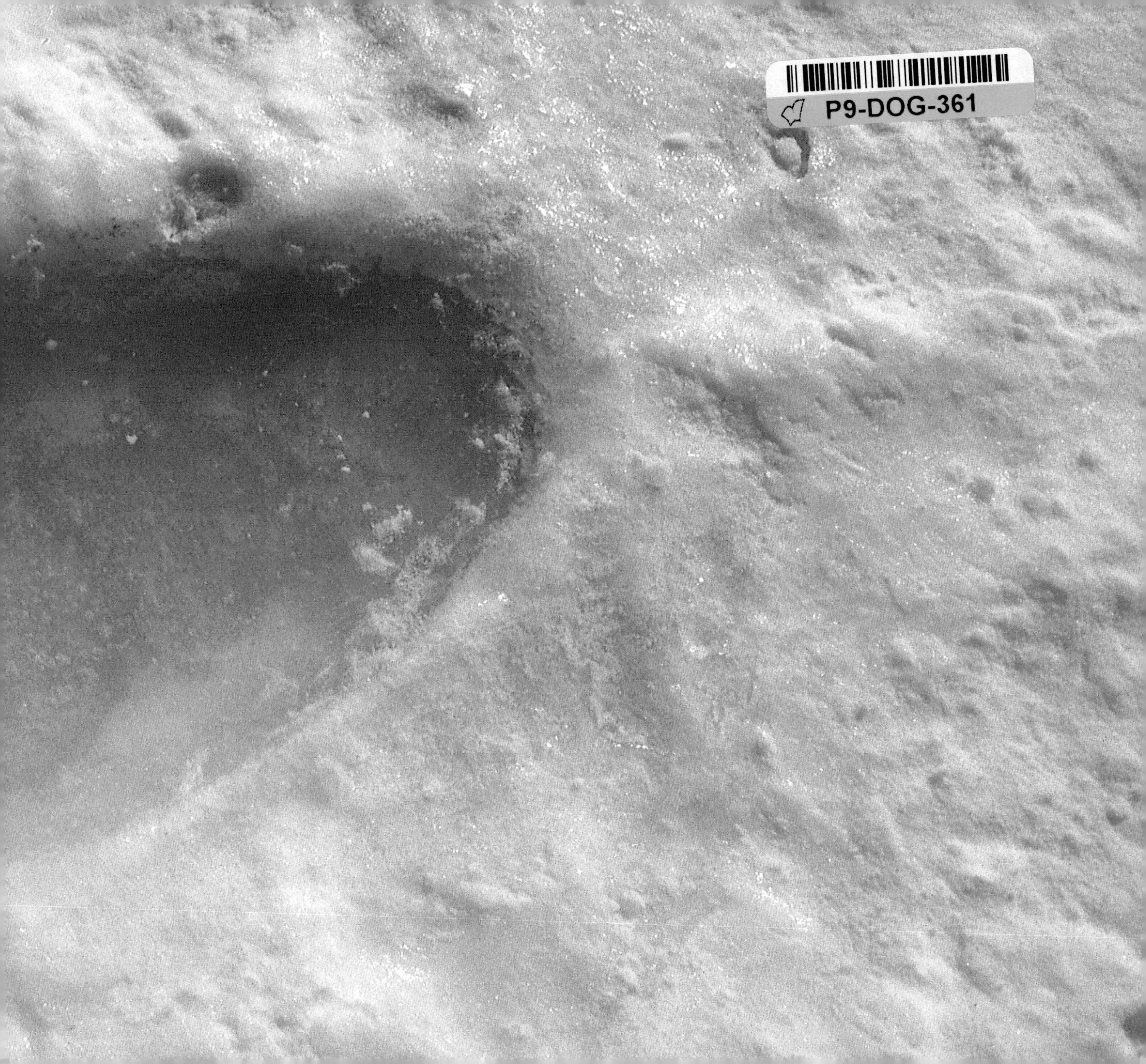

previous pages/A harp seal pup's bed
is made of ice. The depression melted
into the ice from a pup's body temperature
is called an *ice cradle*.

Executive Editor/Seiji Horibuchi
Translator/Yuji Oniki
Art Direction/Shinji Horibuchi & Tokiko Tsumemaru
Publisher/Keizo Inoue

© 1996 by Mitsuaki Iwago

Printed in Japan

Originally published as *Kôrimo Yurikago*
by Shogakukan, Inc. in Japan
Art Direction/Keisuke Konishi
Map/Hiroyuki Kimura
Editor/Shuji Shimamoto

ISBN 1-56931-148-X

First printing, October 1996

Cadence Books
A division of Viz Communications, Inc.
P.O. Box 77010
San Francisco, CA 94107

Helen E

HARP SEAL BABY BOOK

Three Weeks in an Arctic Nursery

MITSUAKI IWAGO

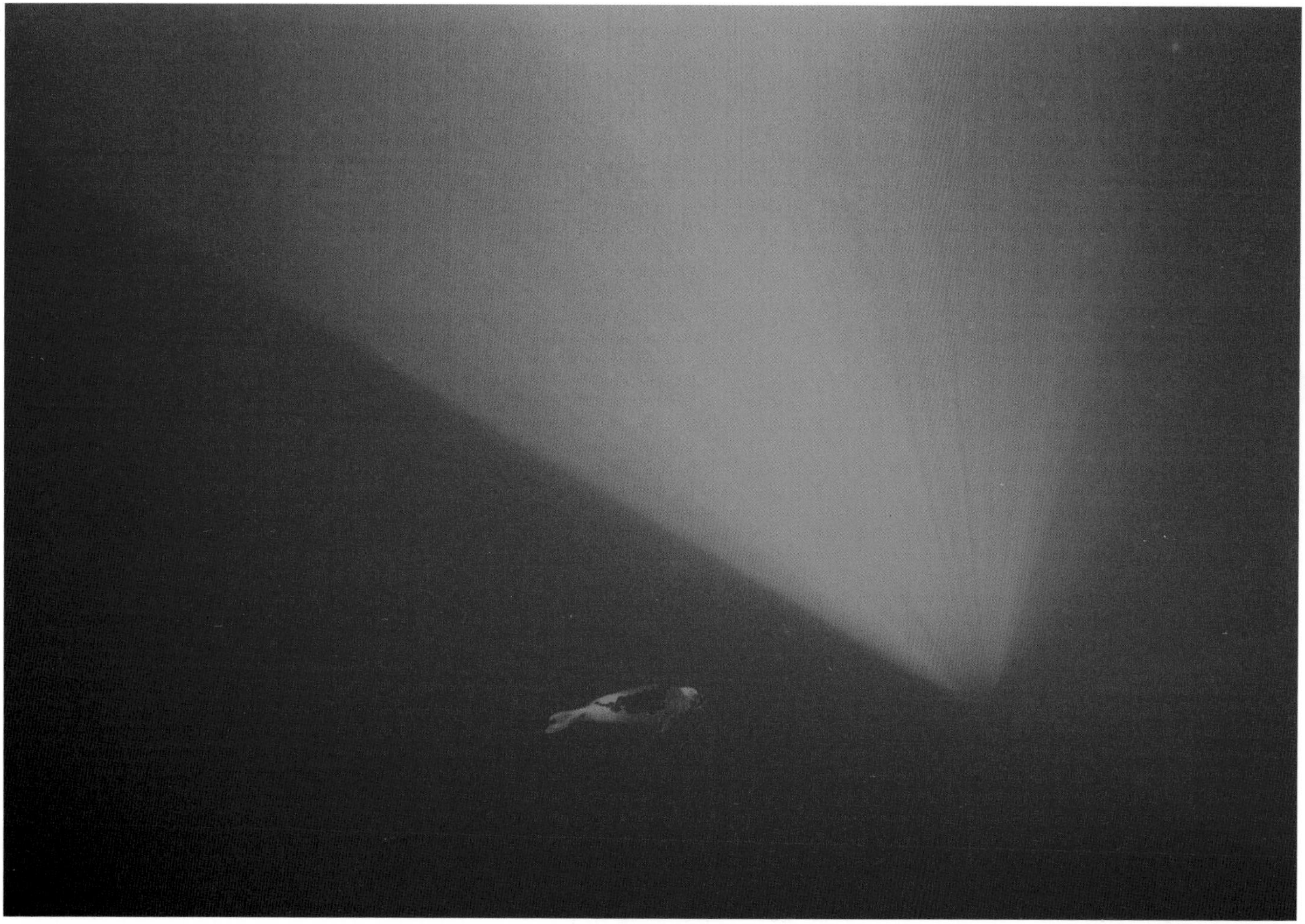

Cadence Books
San Francisco

March first

Harp seals return to their birthplace annually to rear their pups and breed. Pregnant females migrate south from the Arctic regions of Canada and Greenland, grouping together in February in the icy waters off Newfoundland in the Gulf of Saint Lawrence.

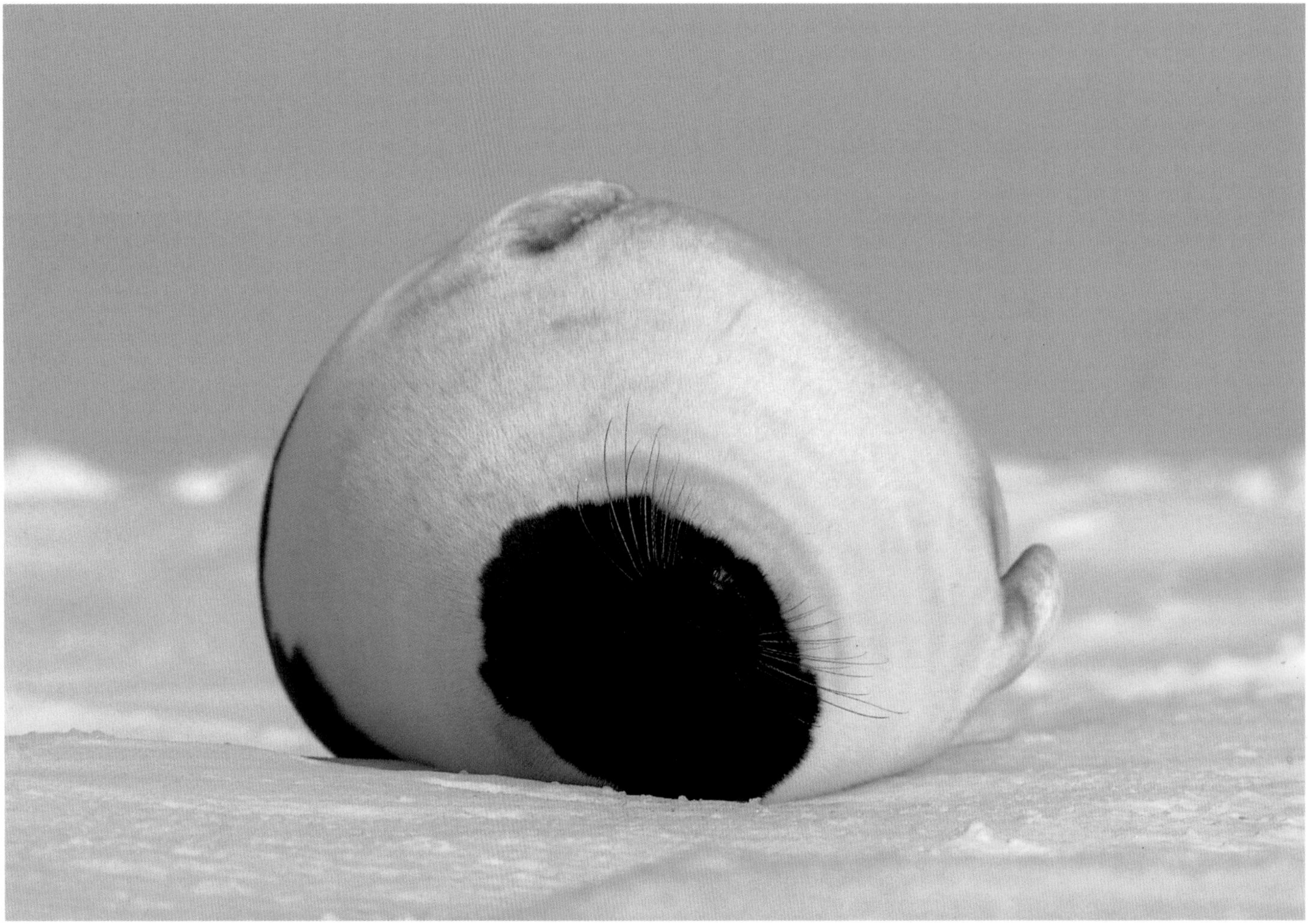

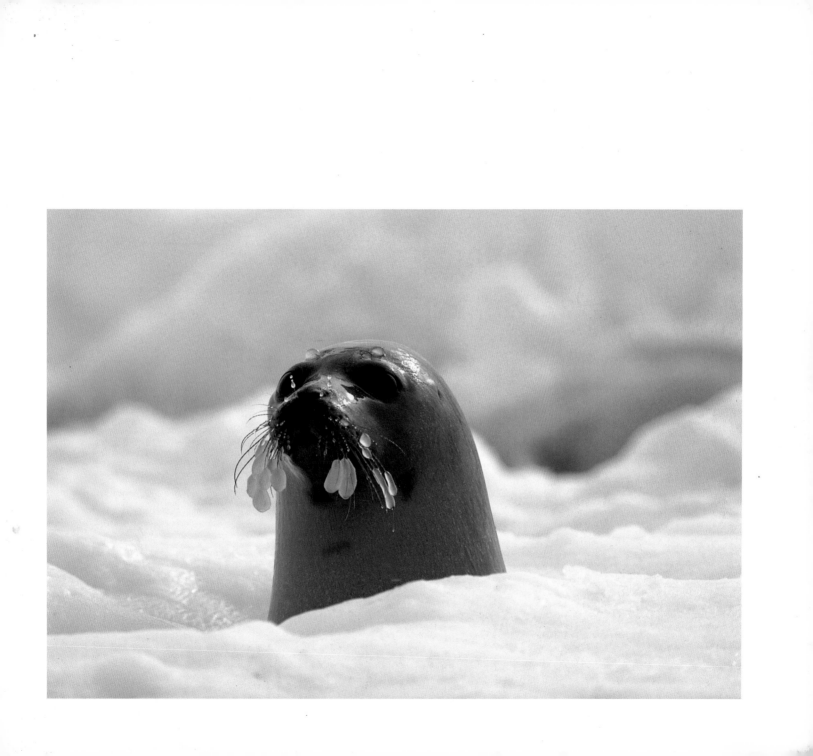

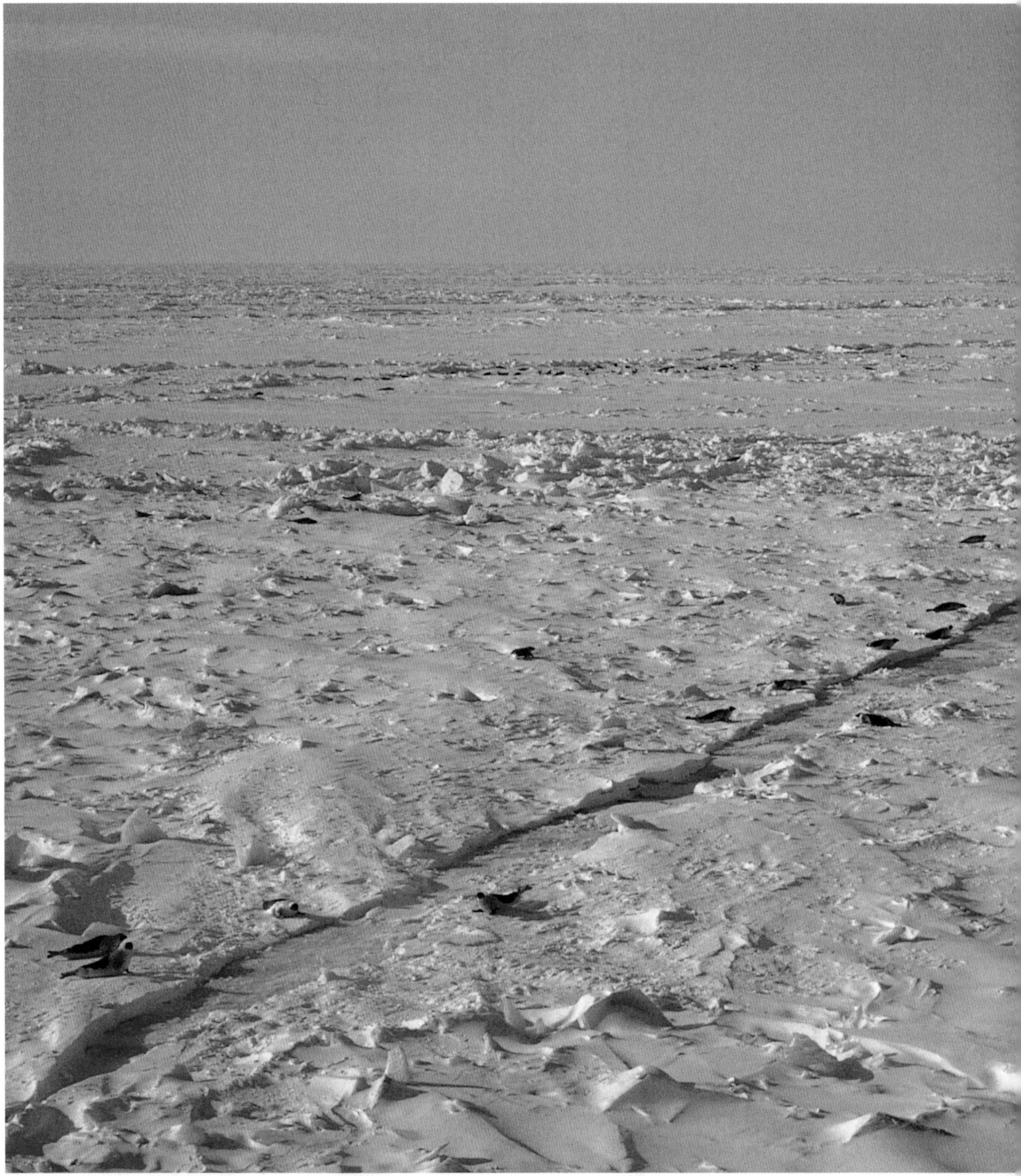

day one

Between the end of February and the middle of March, as the harsh winter gradually comes to an end, 100,000 harp seals give birth to their pups in Canada's Gulf of Saint Lawrence. Emerging from its mother's warm 99°F womb, the newborn seal pup encounters a world with temperatures well below freezing. The mother and pup learn each other's smell immediately. For two days, the mother never leaves her offspring. The pup must be well protected during this period.

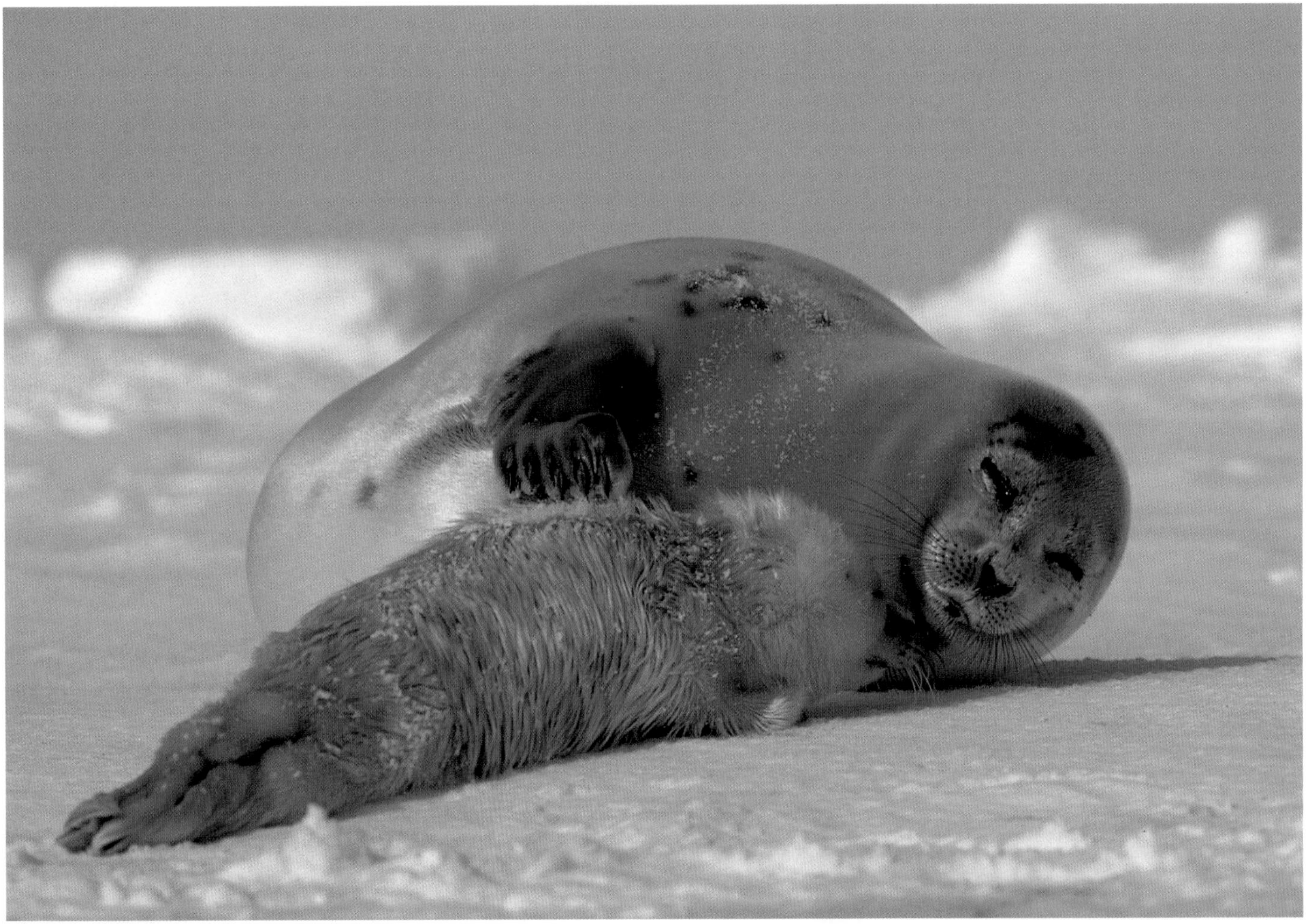

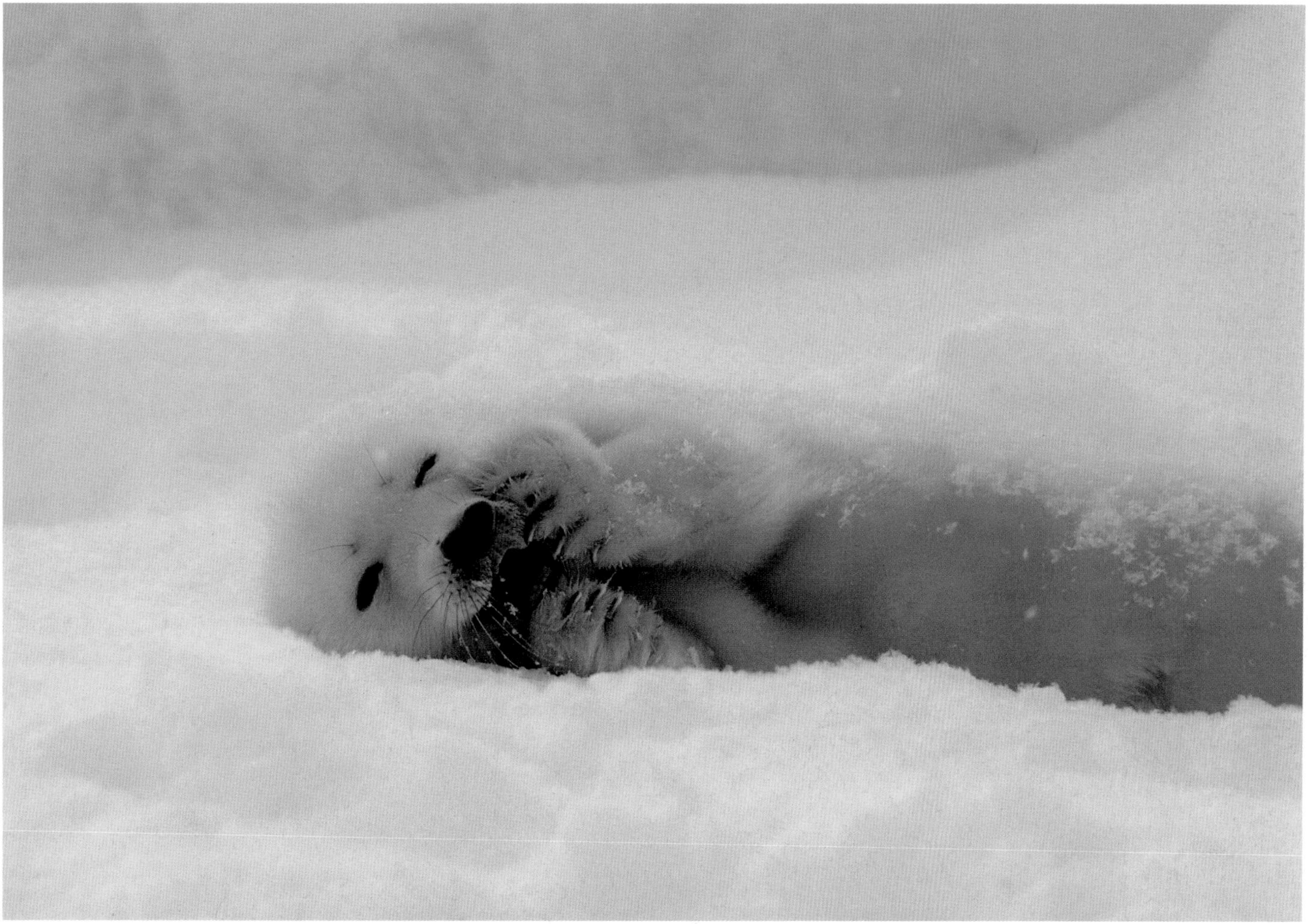

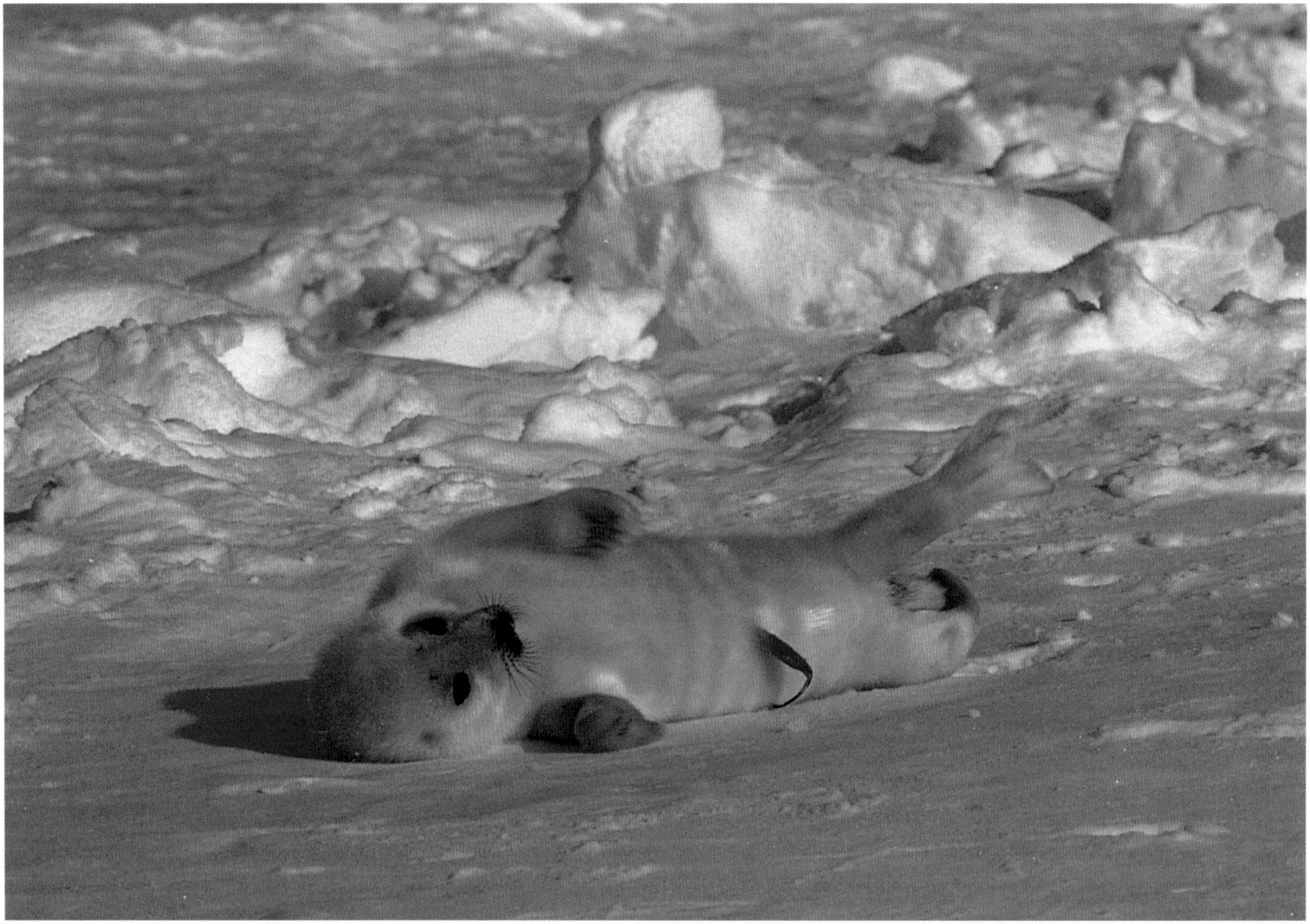

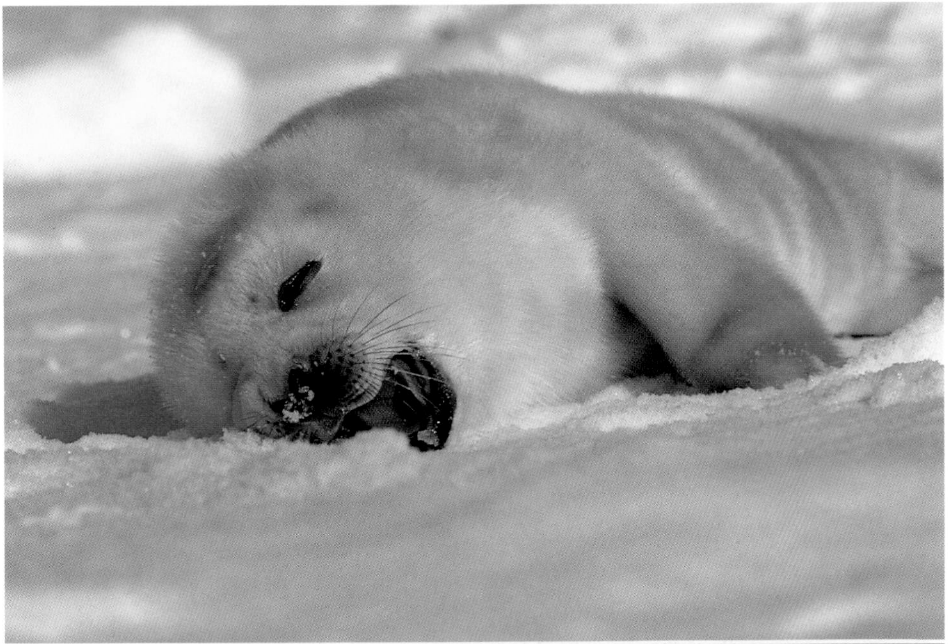
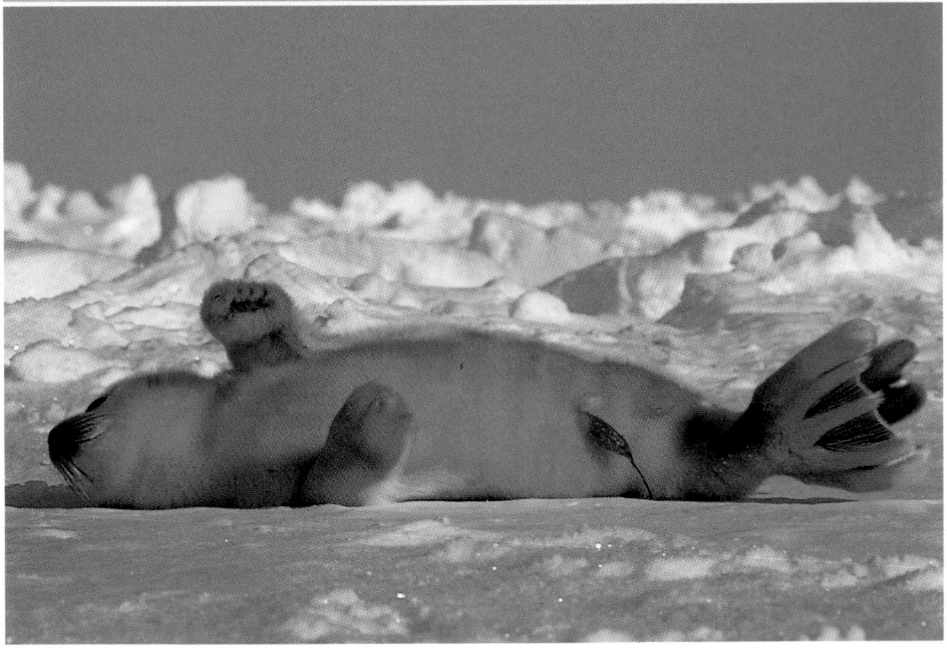

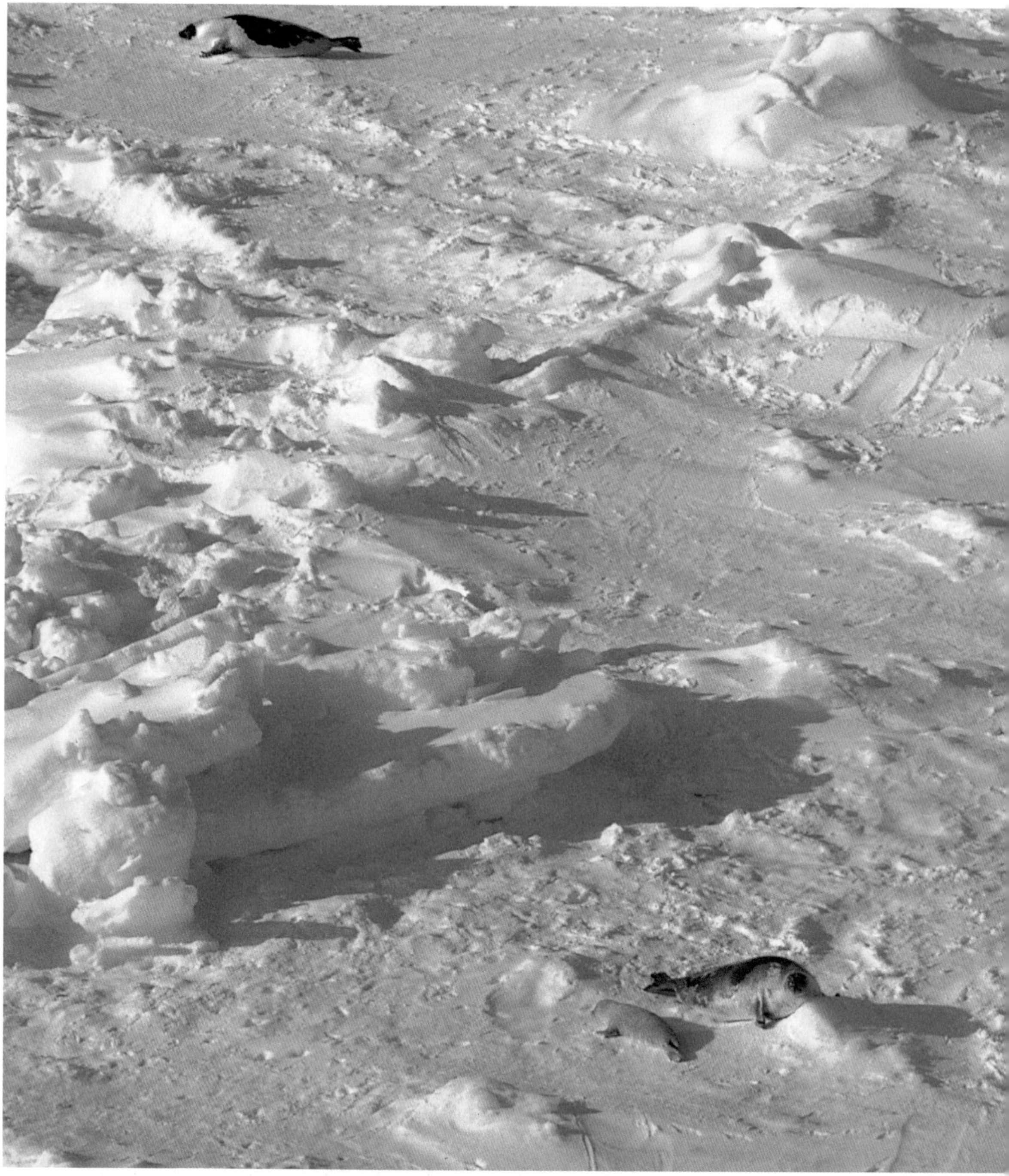

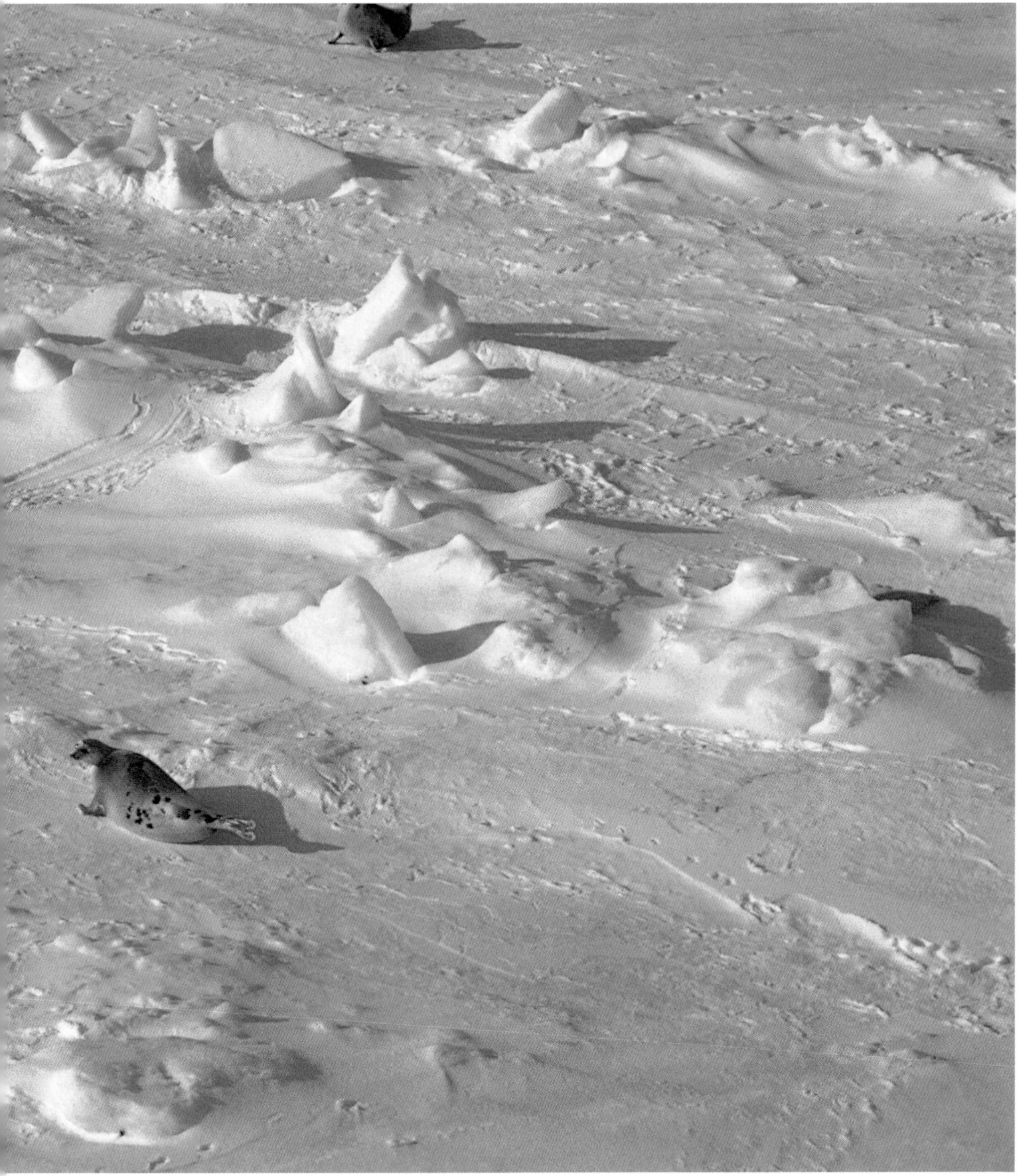

day two

The seal pup's fur, shining brightly in the sun, is a golden yellow at first, tinted by the amniotic fluids from the womb. Poking its small head up, it searches for its mother's teats. First the pup finds the hind flippers. Then it tries to suckle on the front flippers. Finally, the mother seal guides her offspring to her teats with her front flippers. The pup suckles clumsily in the beginning, but by the second day it won't let go and nurses continually.

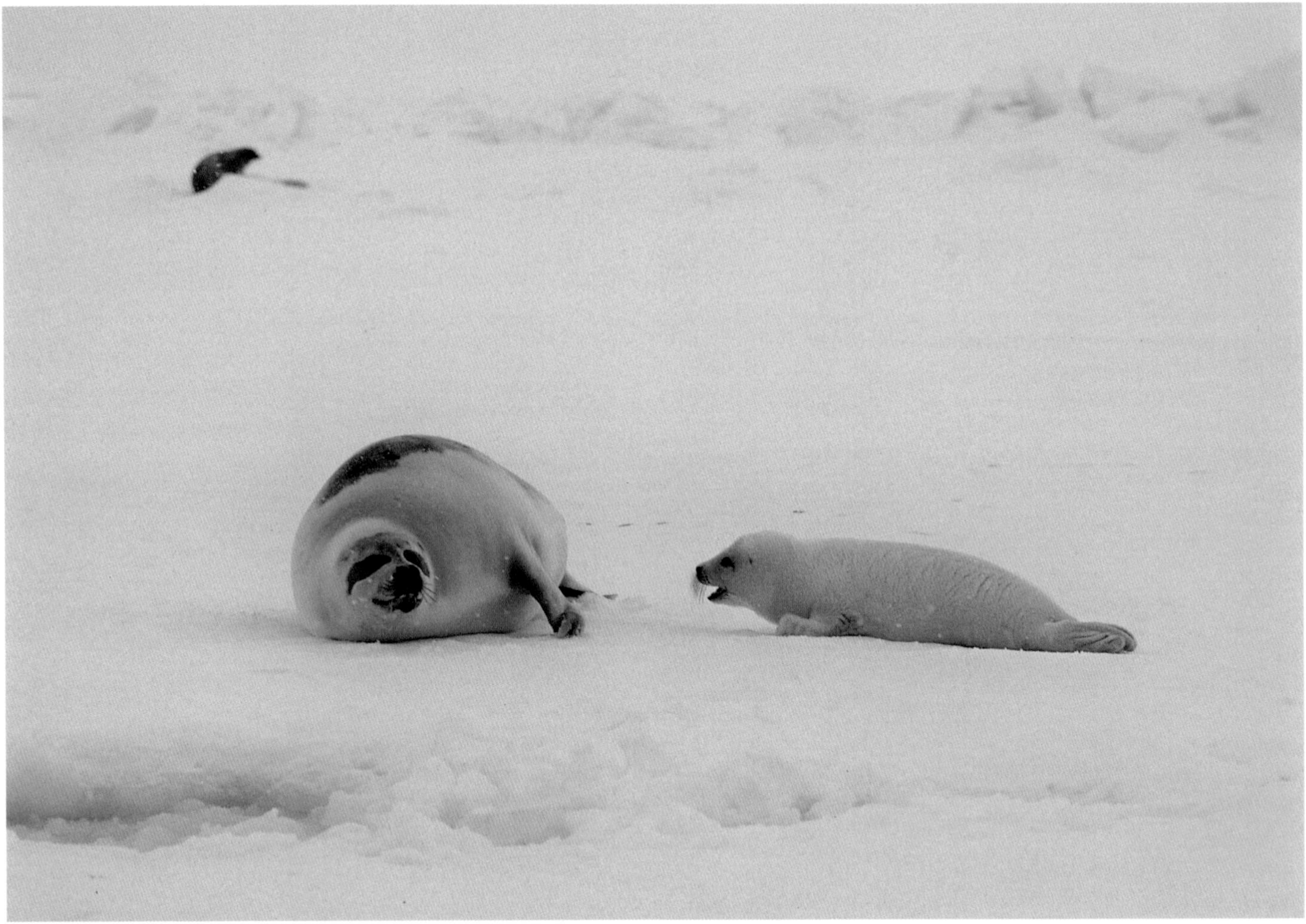

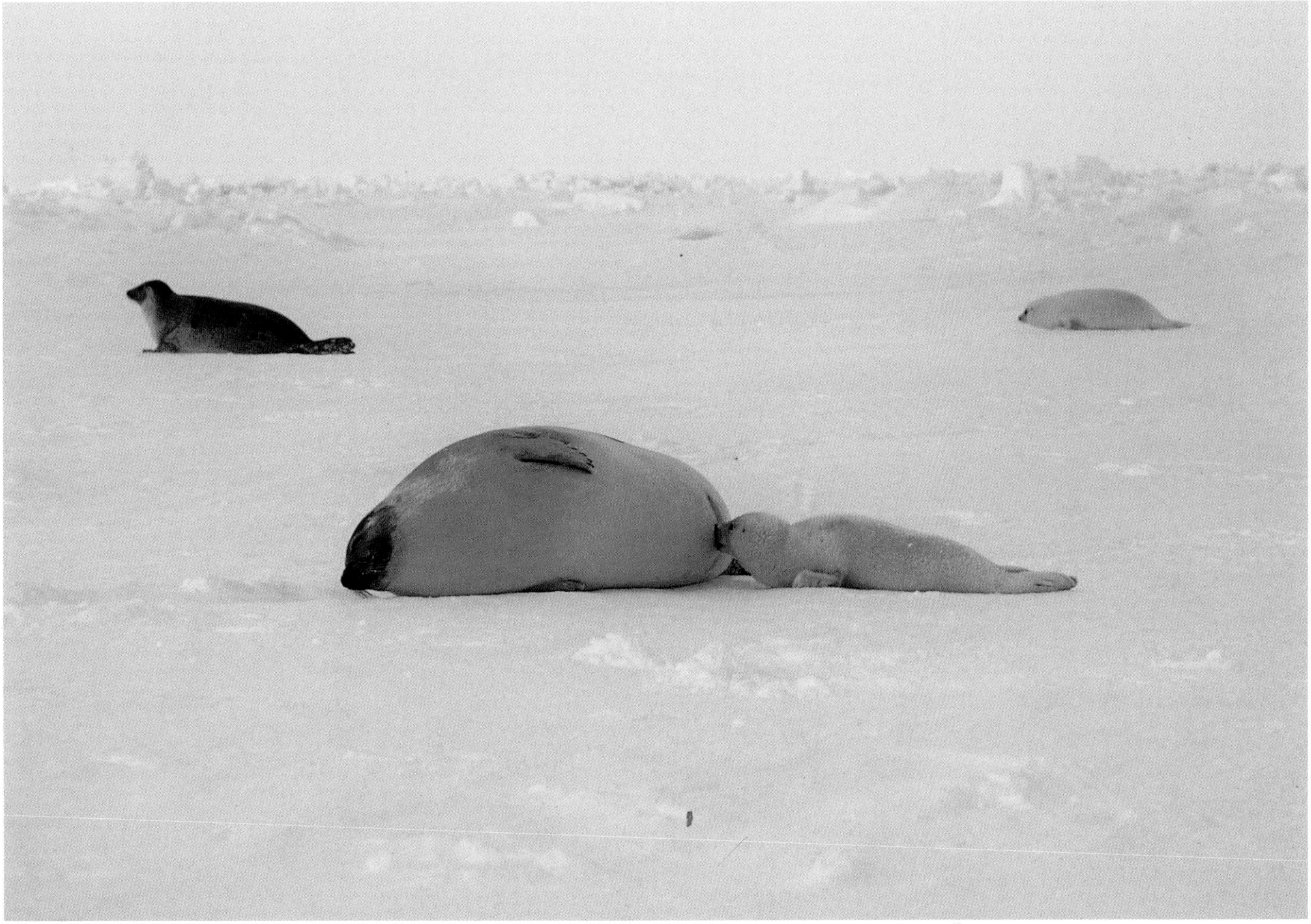

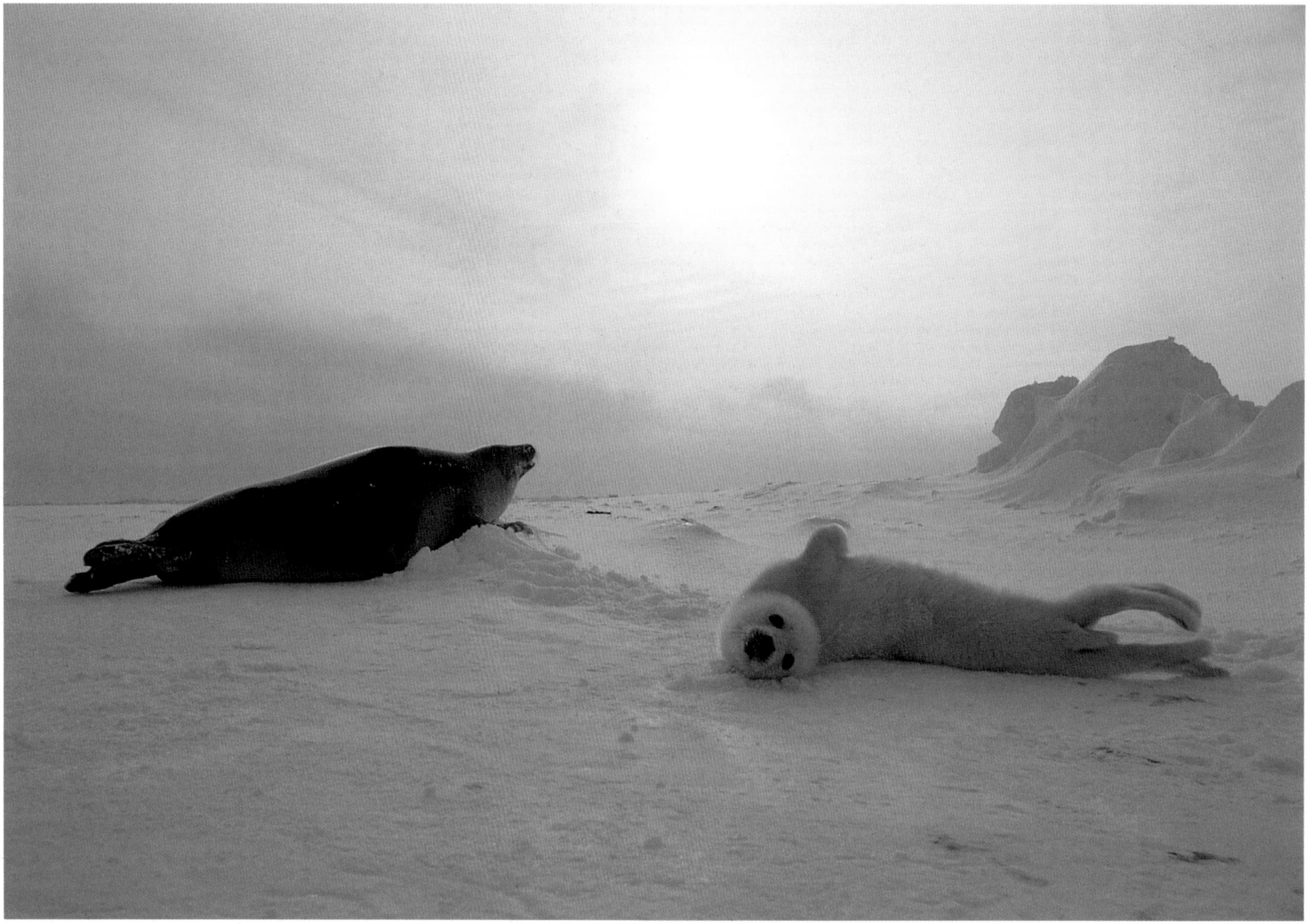

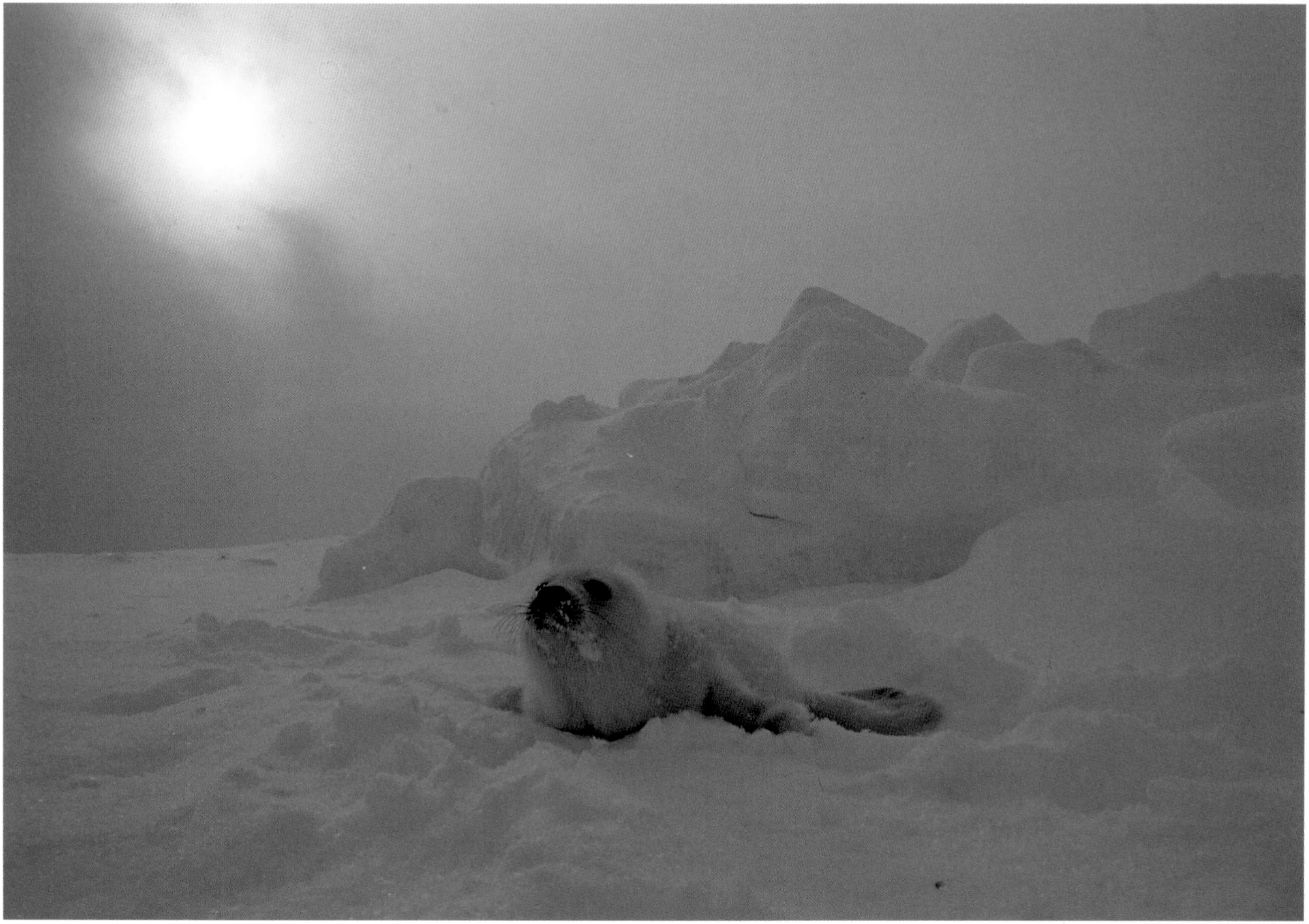

day three

Our helicopter flies over the frozen
water. It's a clear day, and the horizon
marks the border between the blue
and white spreading out endlessly
before us. A herd of harp seals appears
below me. It's cold and clear today,
but when the weather gets harsh
everything turns white and we have
to cancel our flight. It's called a "white-
out" when you can't tell the difference
between the sea and sky. For several
days we're unable to fly. Depending on
the tide and winds, the ice flows move
tens of miles in a matter of days. The
harp seals will be somewhere else by
tomorrow.

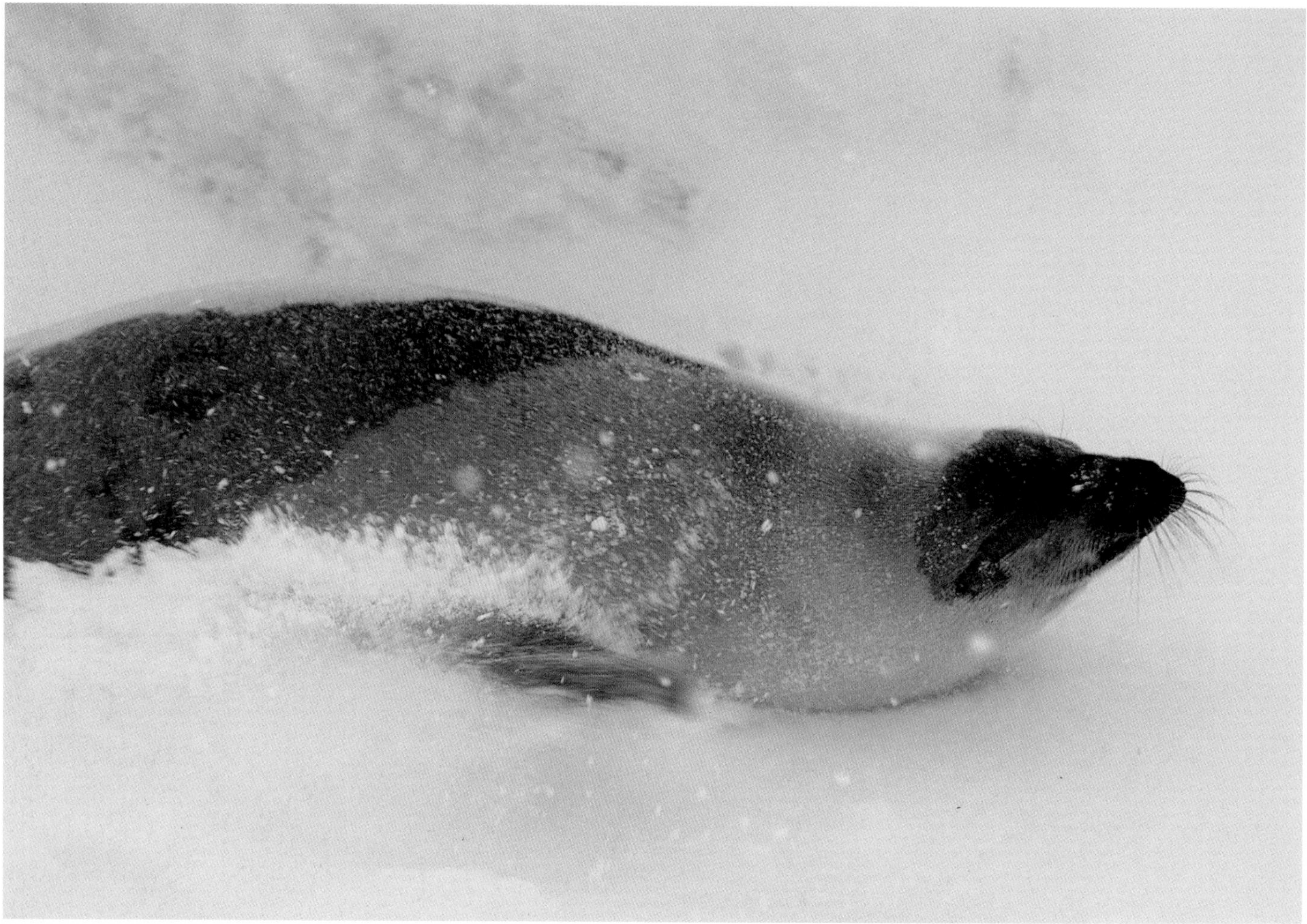

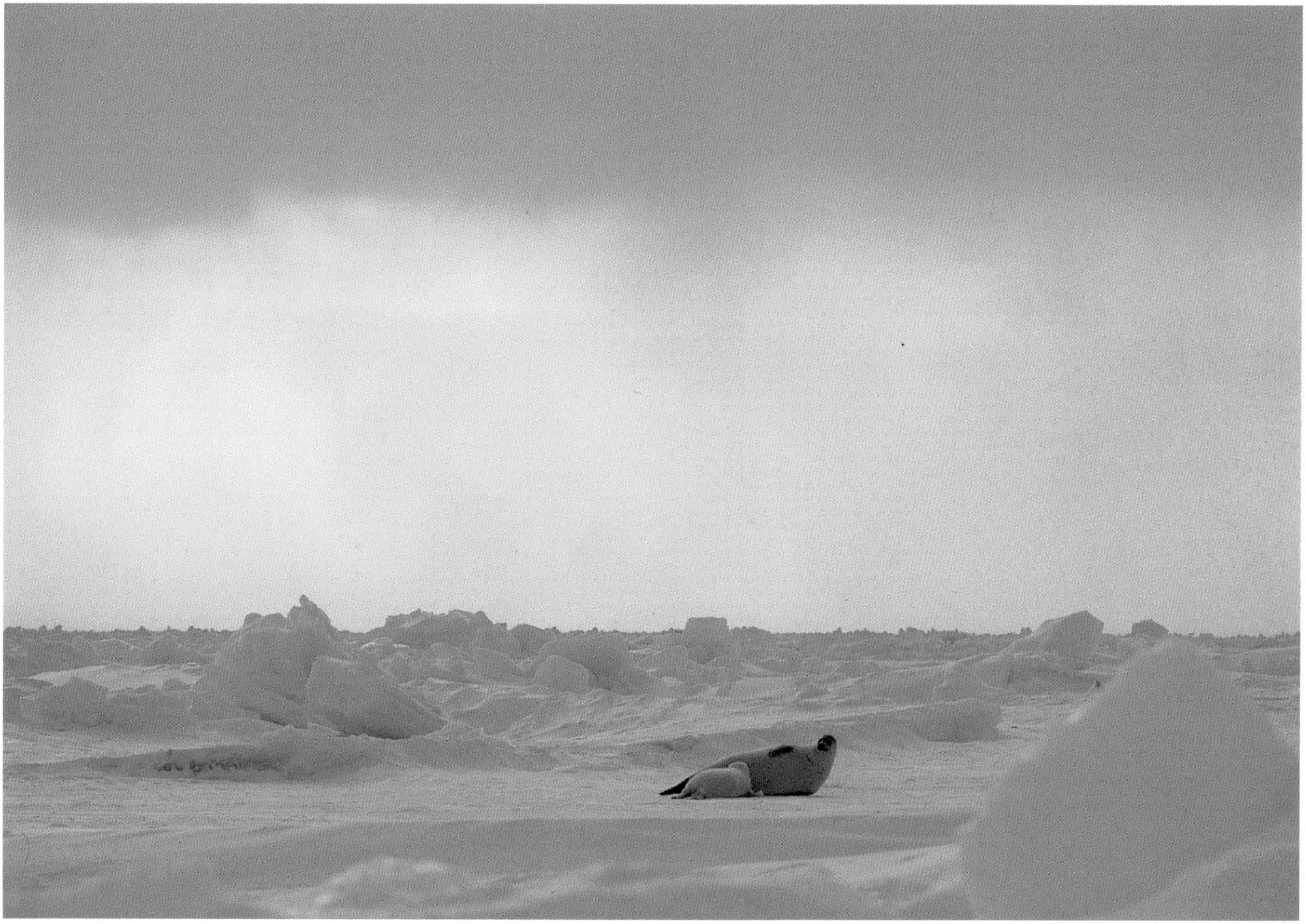

day four

The pup's yellow fur turns white as the pup grows, gaining about four pounds every day. Harp seal milk contains ten times more fat than cow milk. As soon as a feeding is over, the mother seal slips through a hole in the ice, diving into the sea. The paths leading to these holes become etched into the ice.

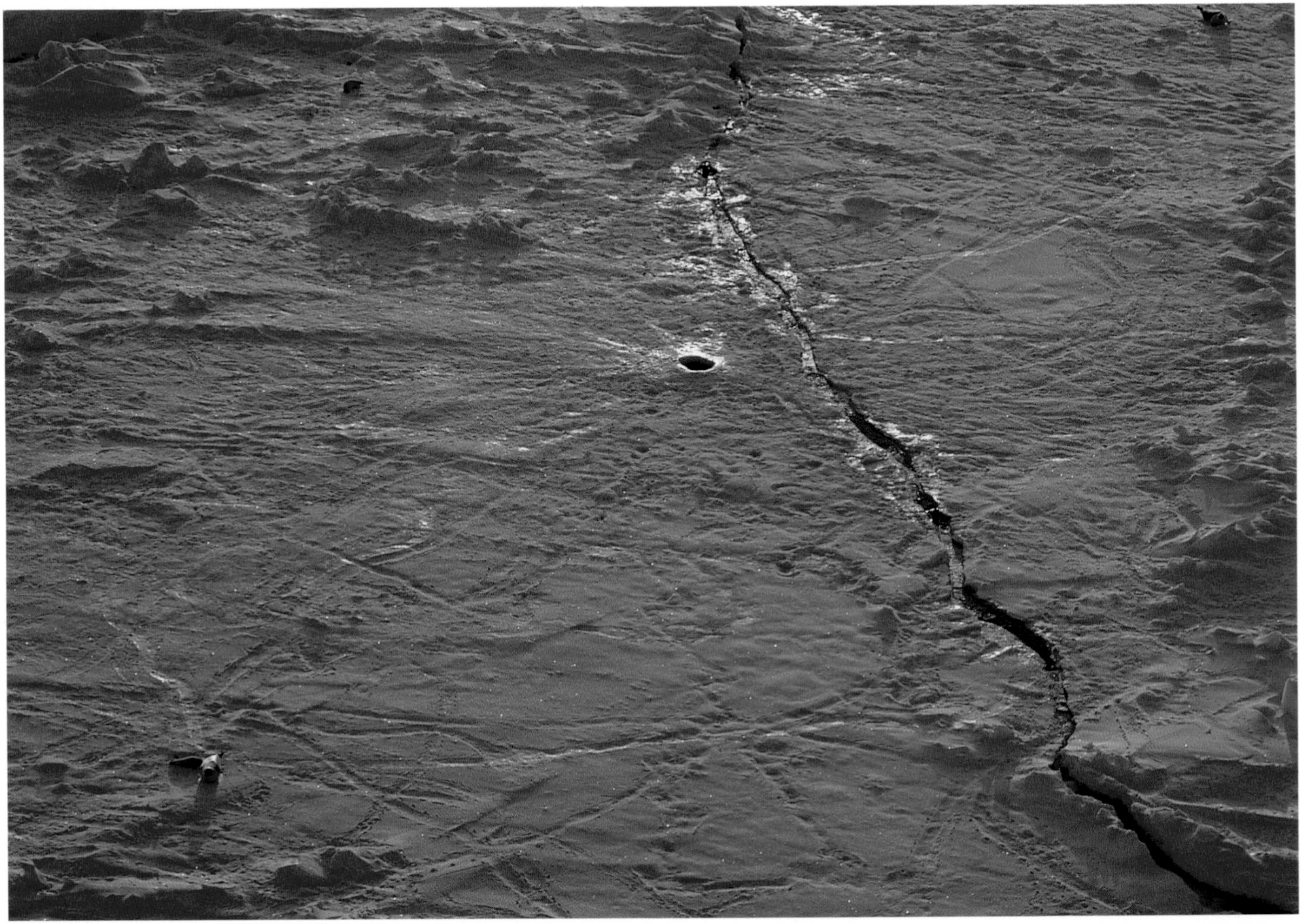

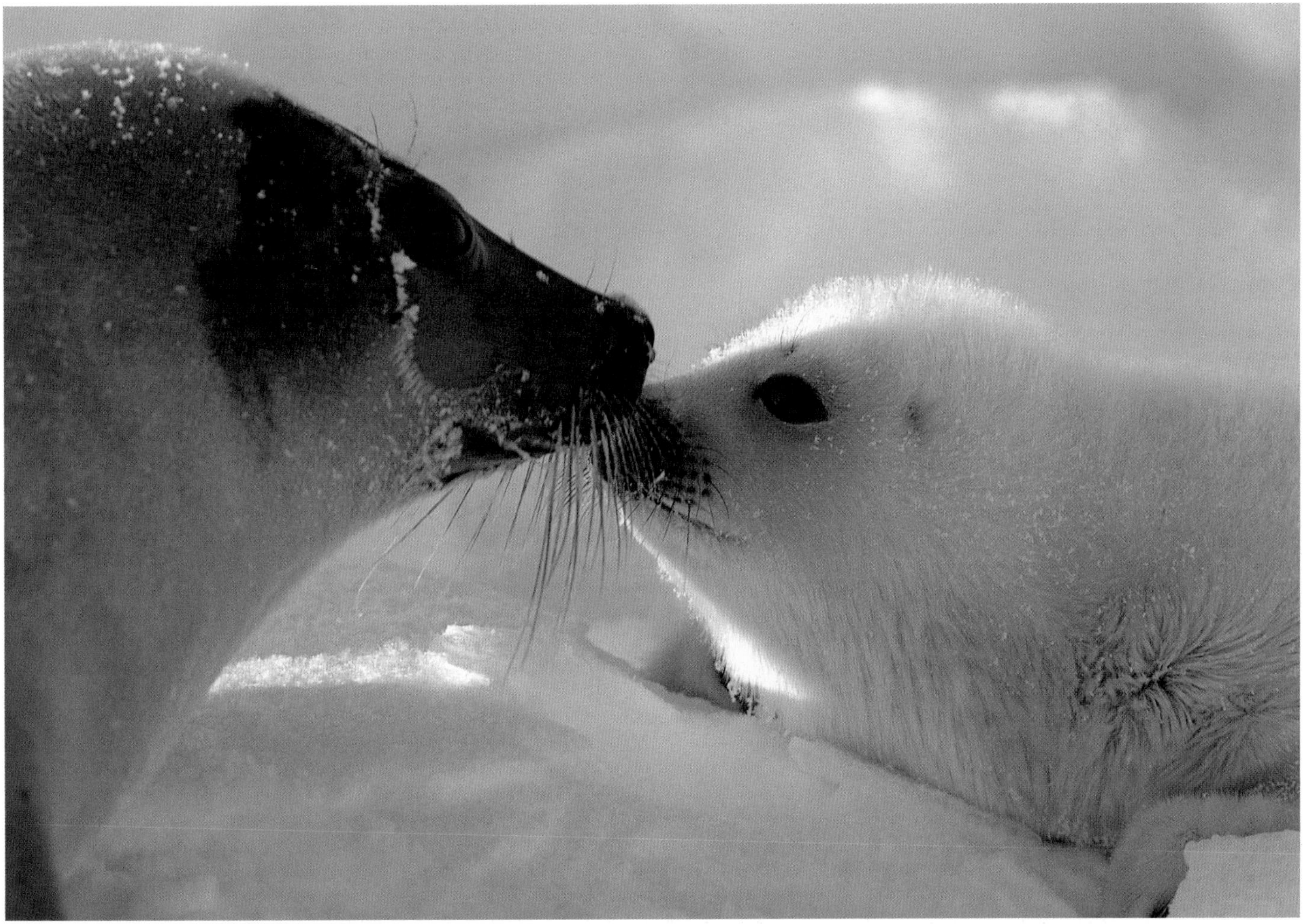

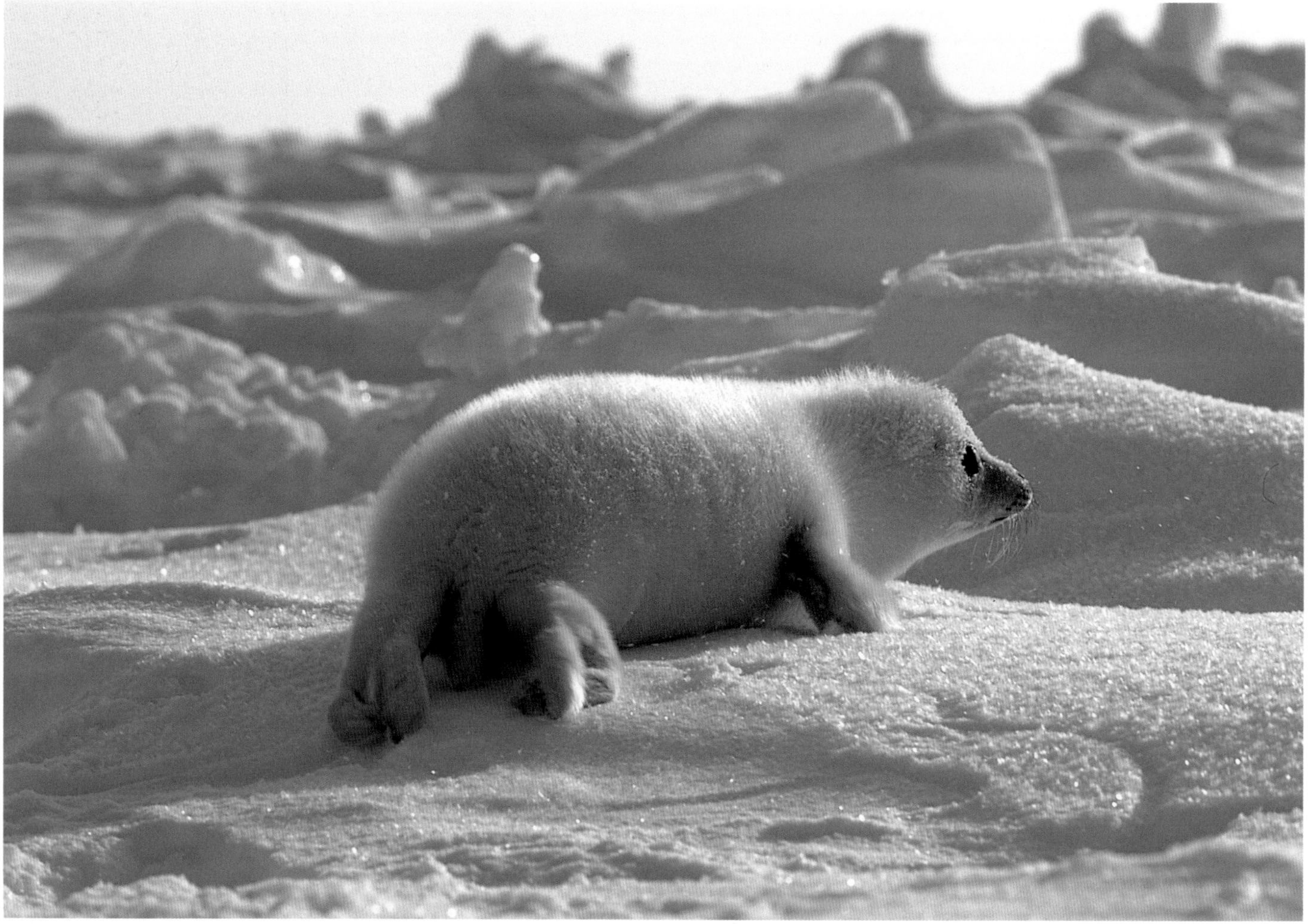

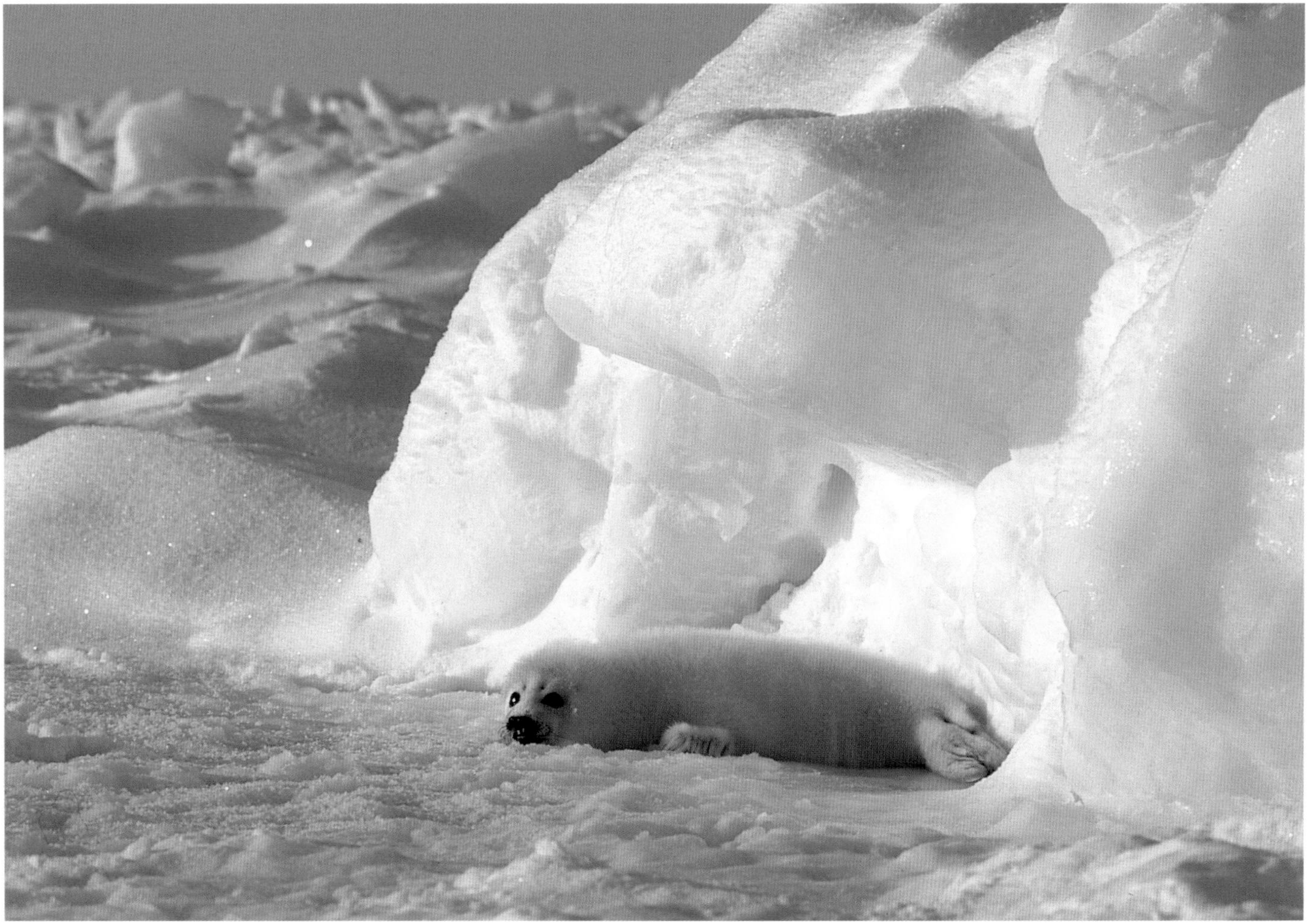

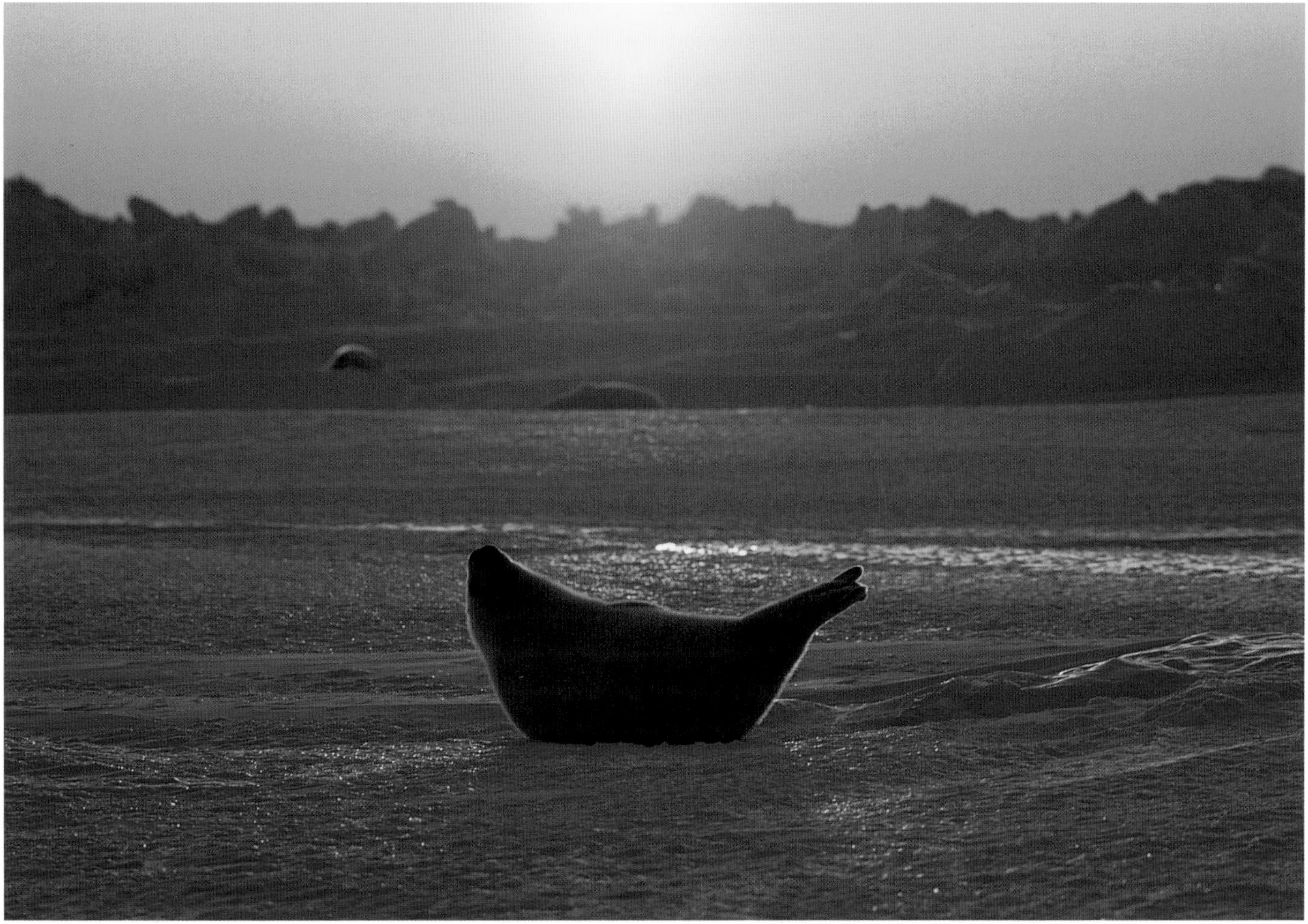

day five

The pup grows as it sleeps. It sleeps through most of the day, in one or two favorite spots where it can avoid the wind. Lying completely still, the pup's body temperature melts the ice away, forming a comfortable ice cradle. As it begins to snow, the landscape changes. The pup flounders forward, crying, in pursuit of its mother.

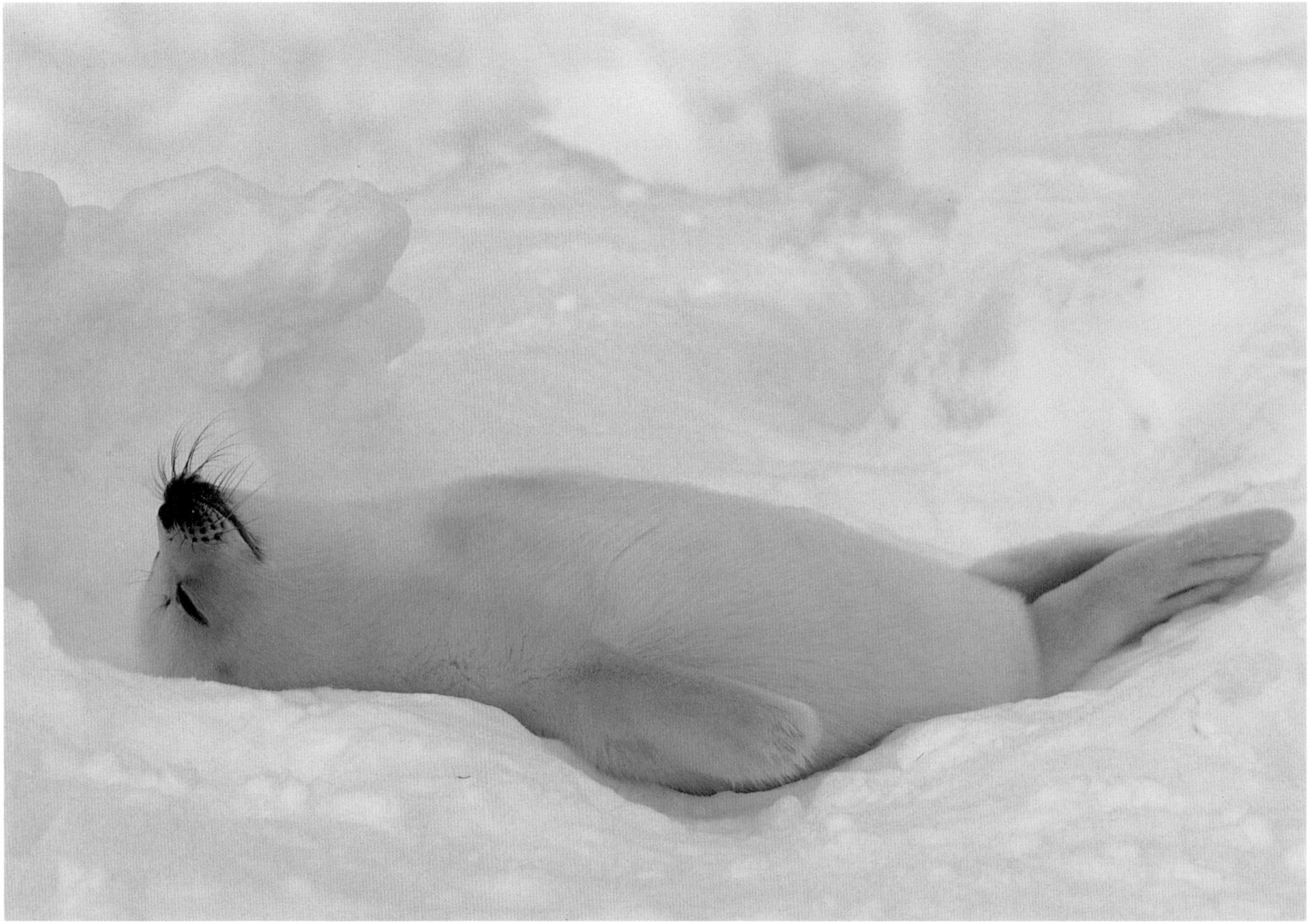

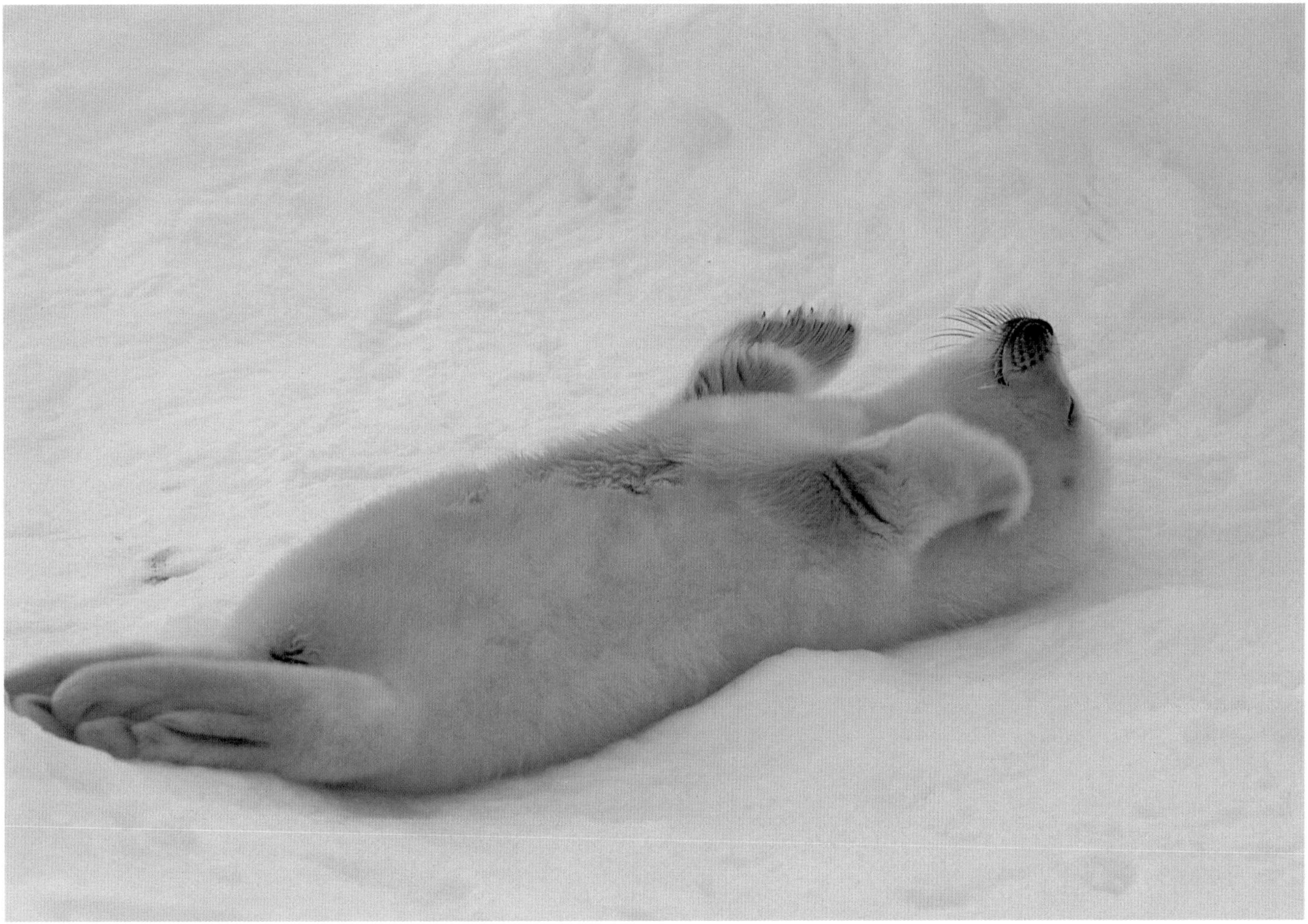

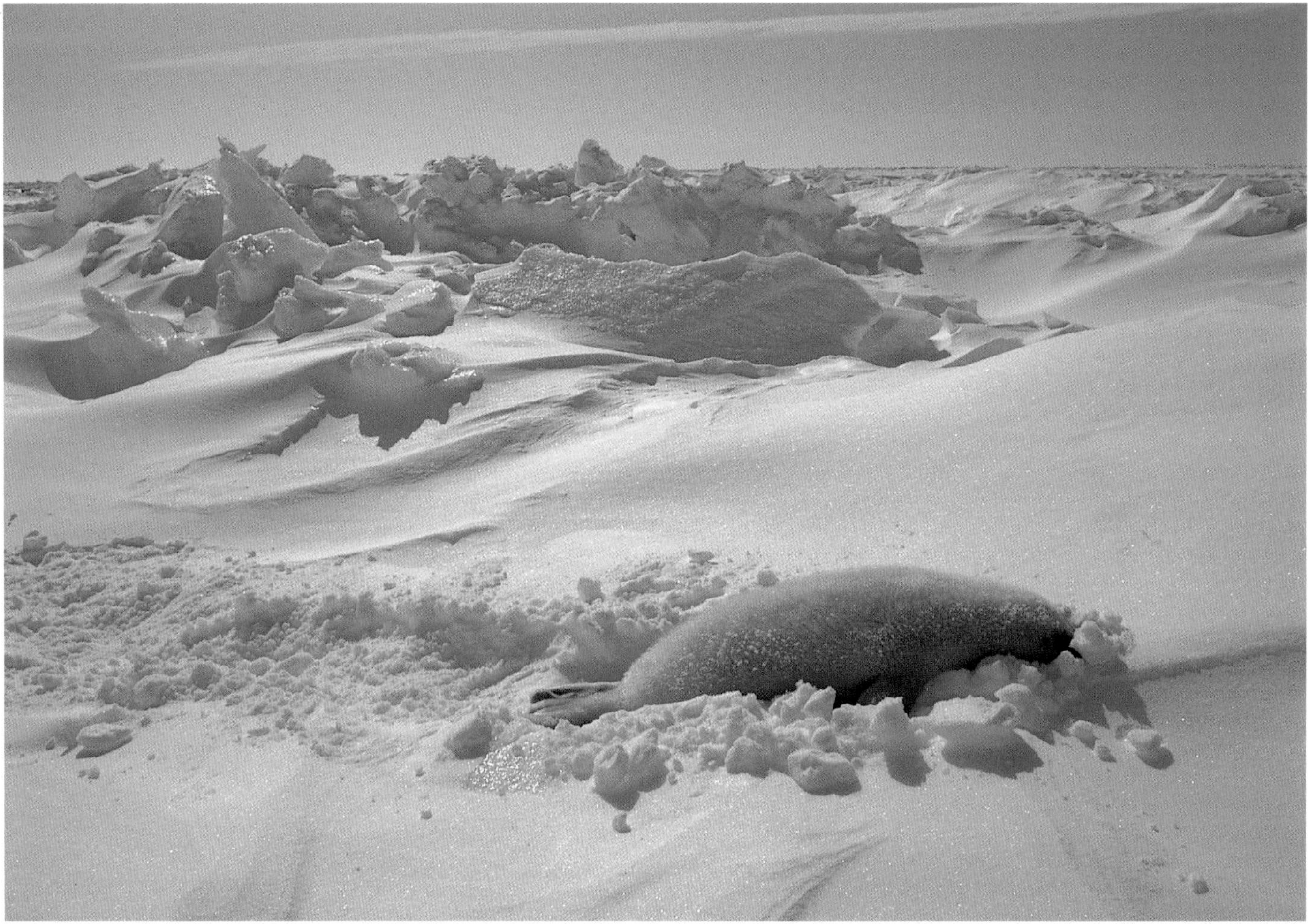

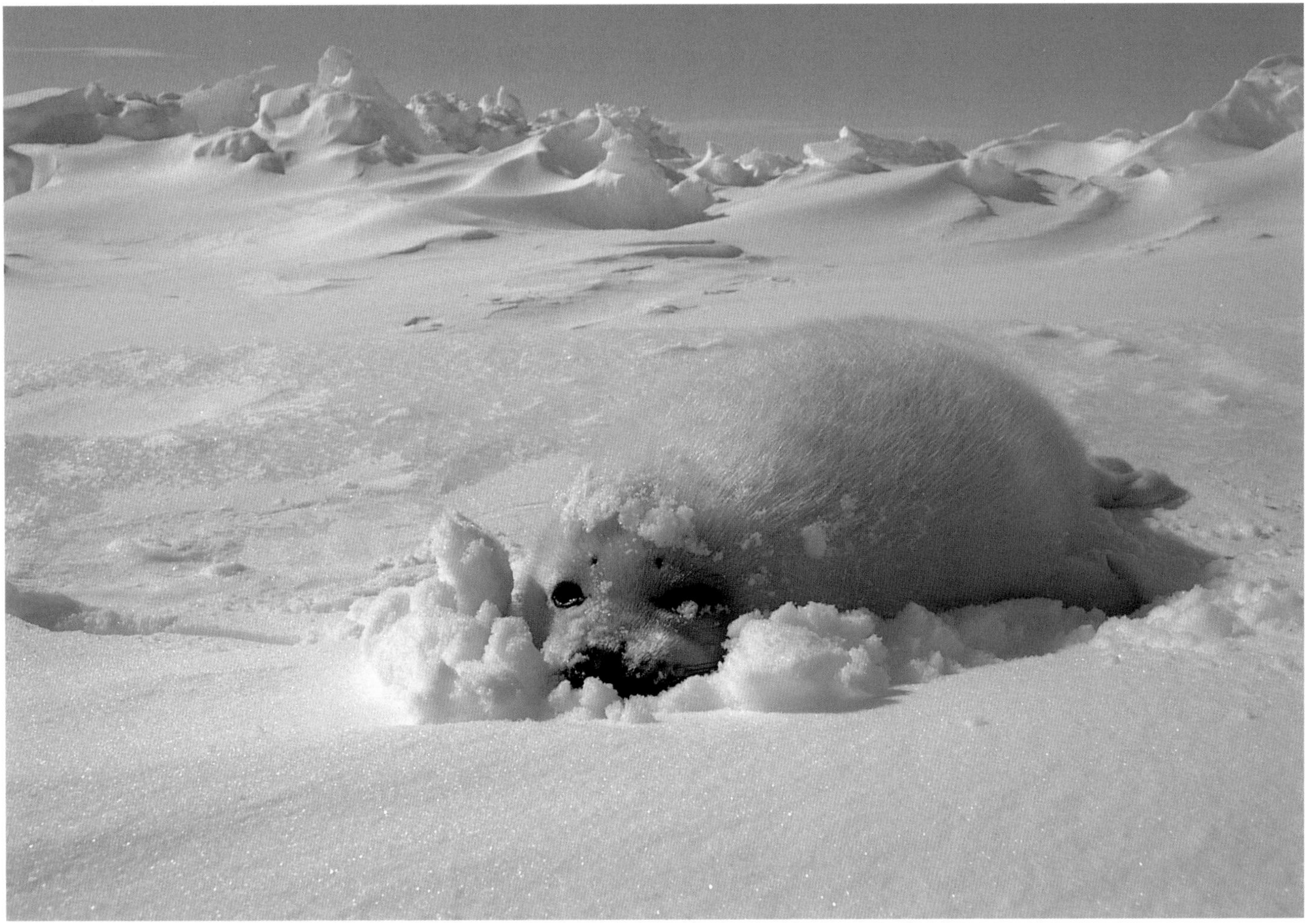

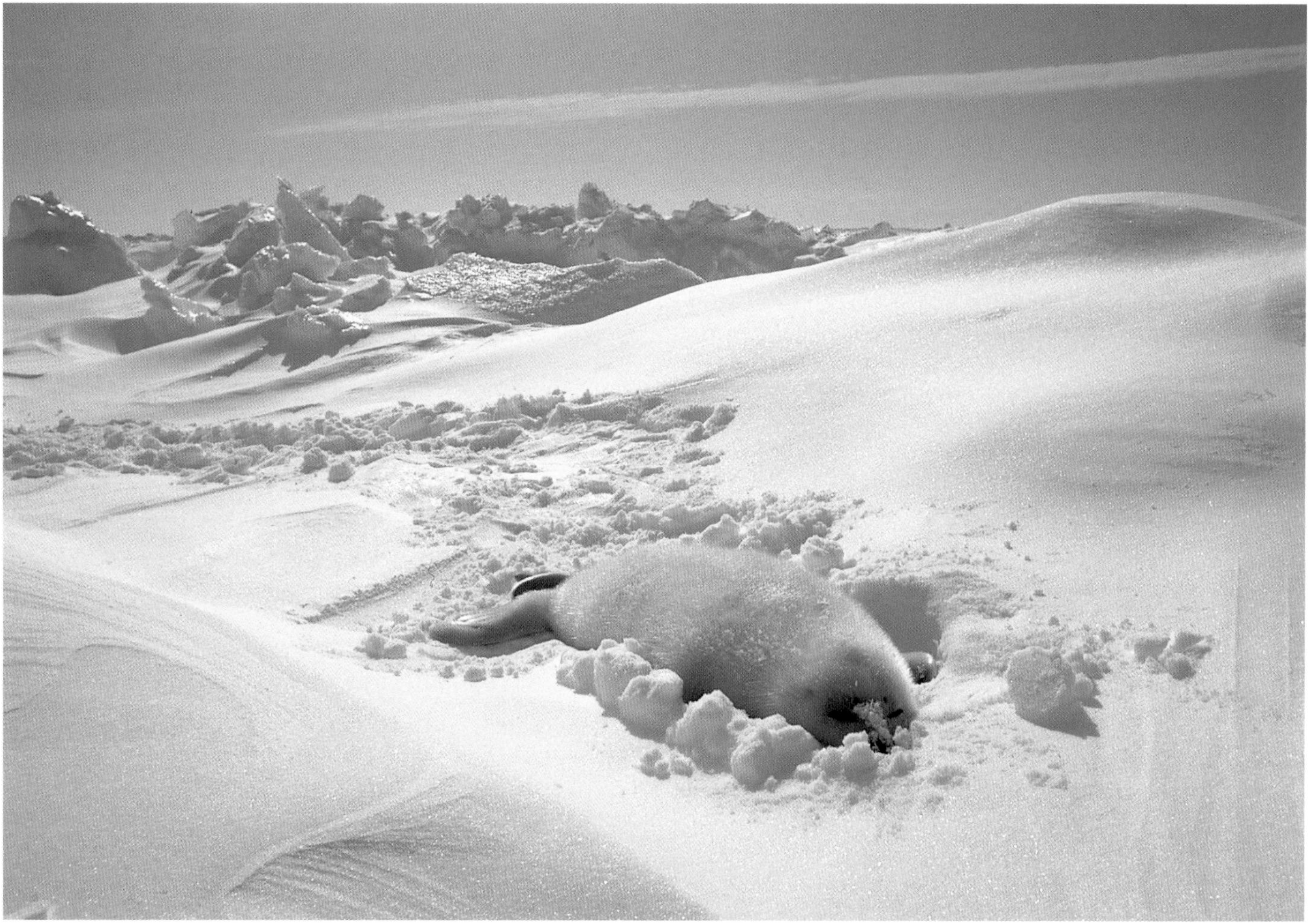

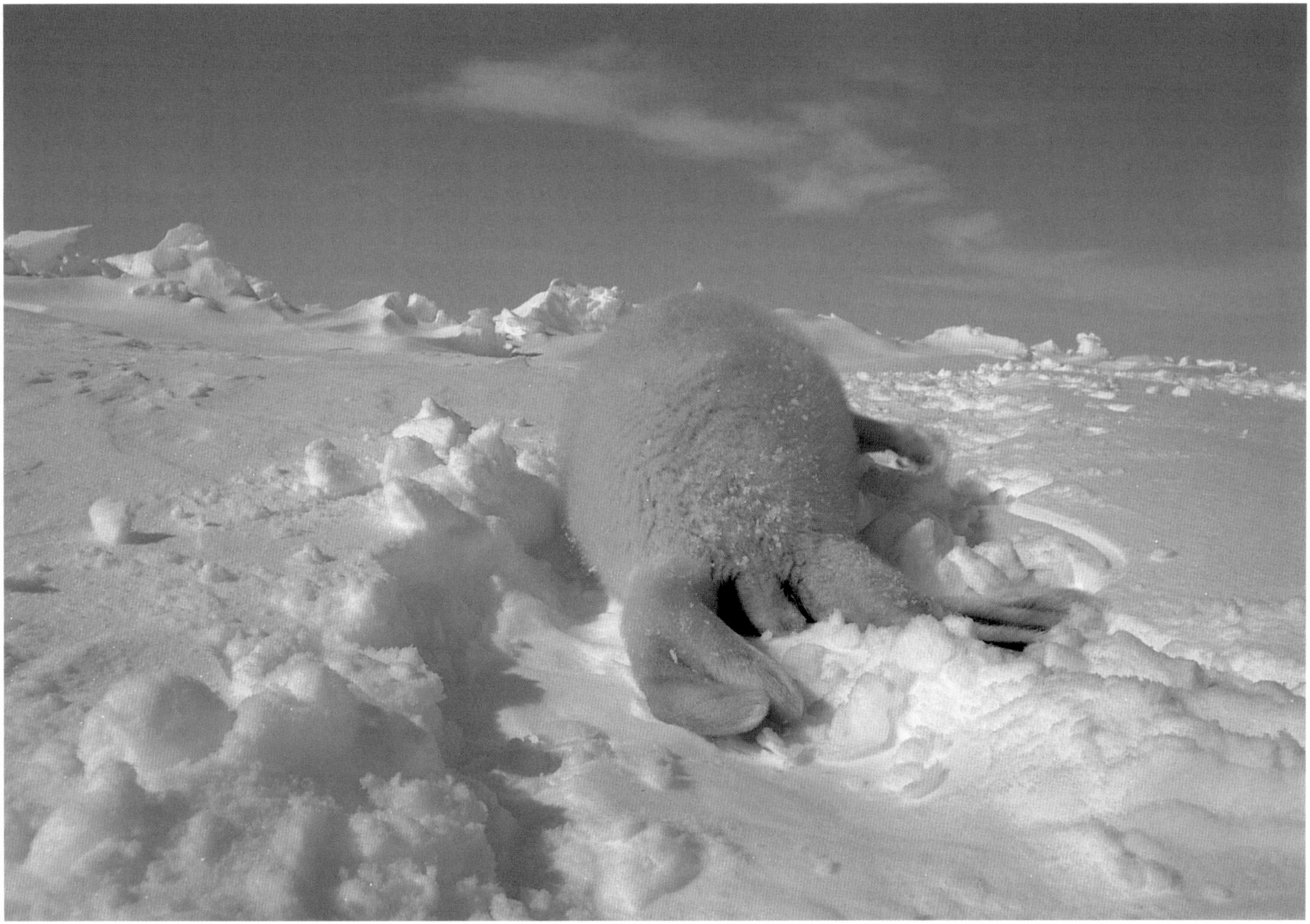

day six

While the female seals raise their pups, the males form separate groups. Soon they begin performing courtship displays, swimming on their backs and blowing water out of their noses. For now, however, the females have no interest in the males. The mother seals often poke their heads out of the ice holes, checking to make sure their pups are safe. If anything approaches their offspring, they respond immediately, sliding over the ice at an incredible speed and baring their teeth to attack the presumed enemy full force.

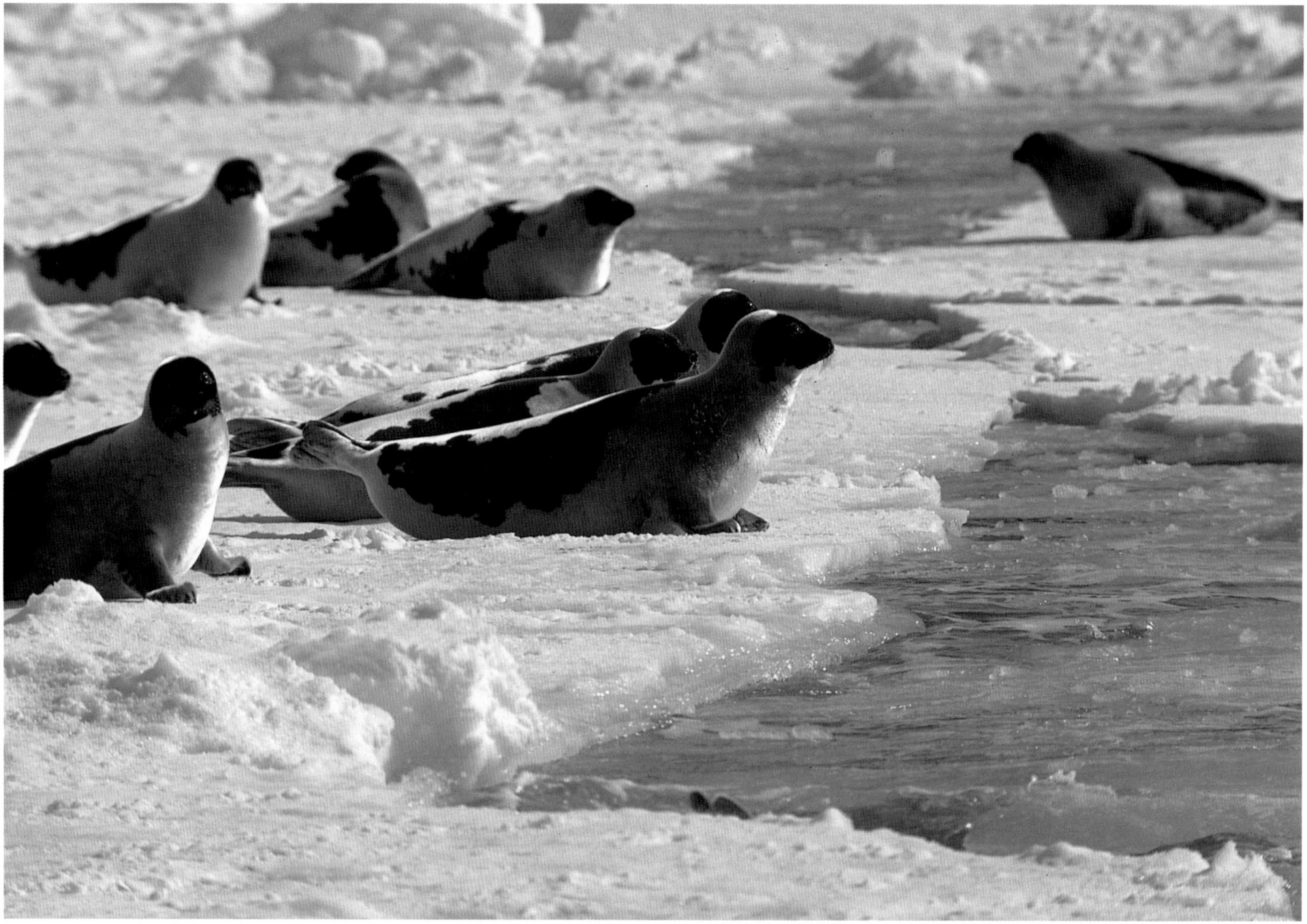

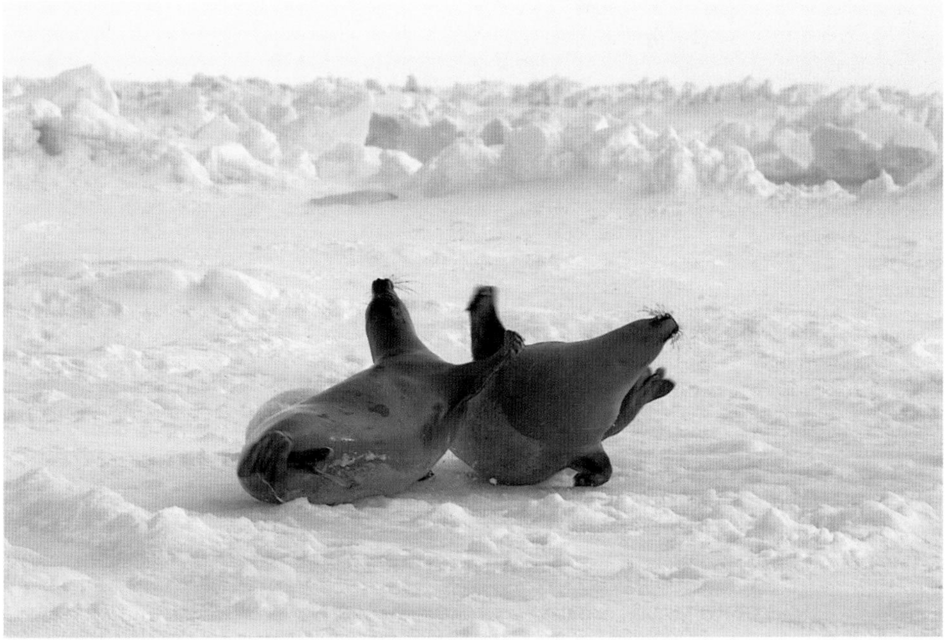

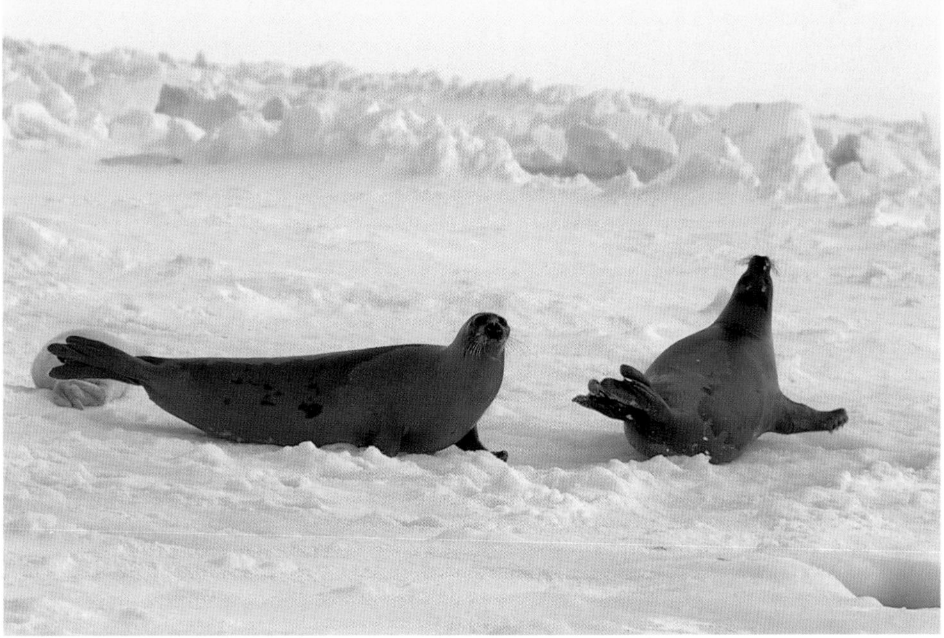

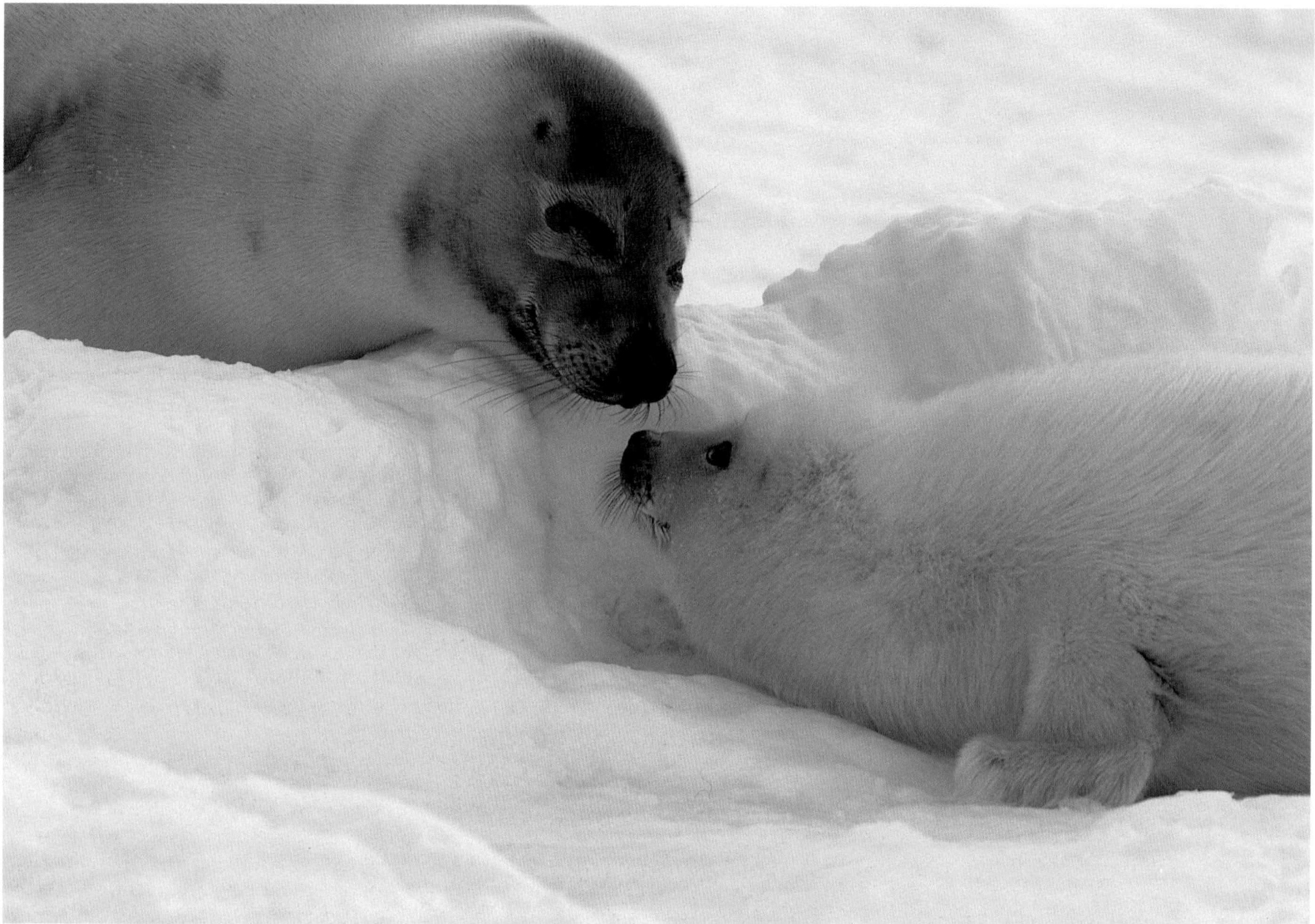

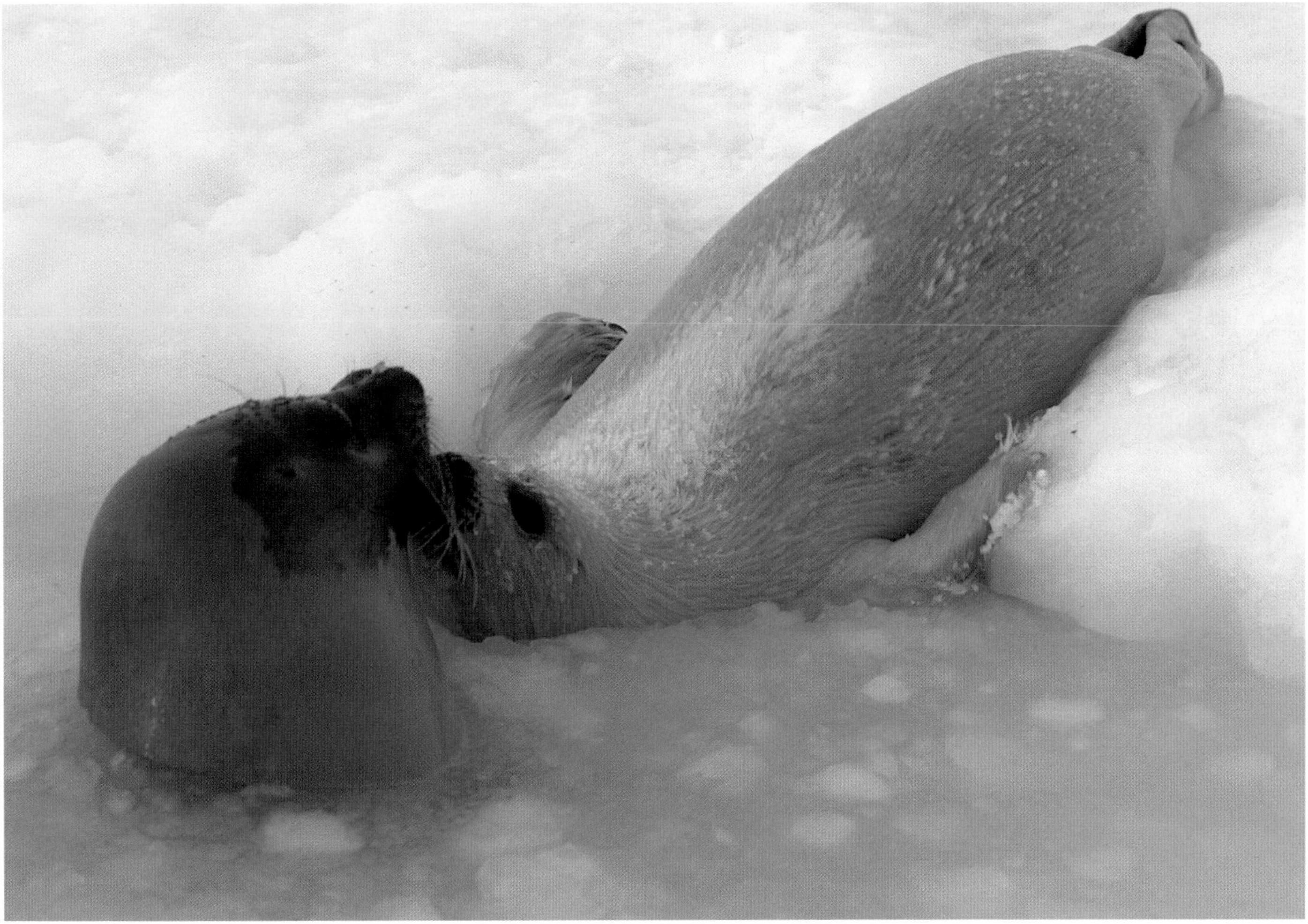

day seven

The adult harp seals spend most of their time in the water under the ice. These sea creatures are quite unusual. The mother seal hardly eats during the nursing period, relying on the blubber she has accumulated during the rest of the year. As a result of burning off this fat to sustain her pup and herself, she loses one-quarter of her weight by the time they separate.

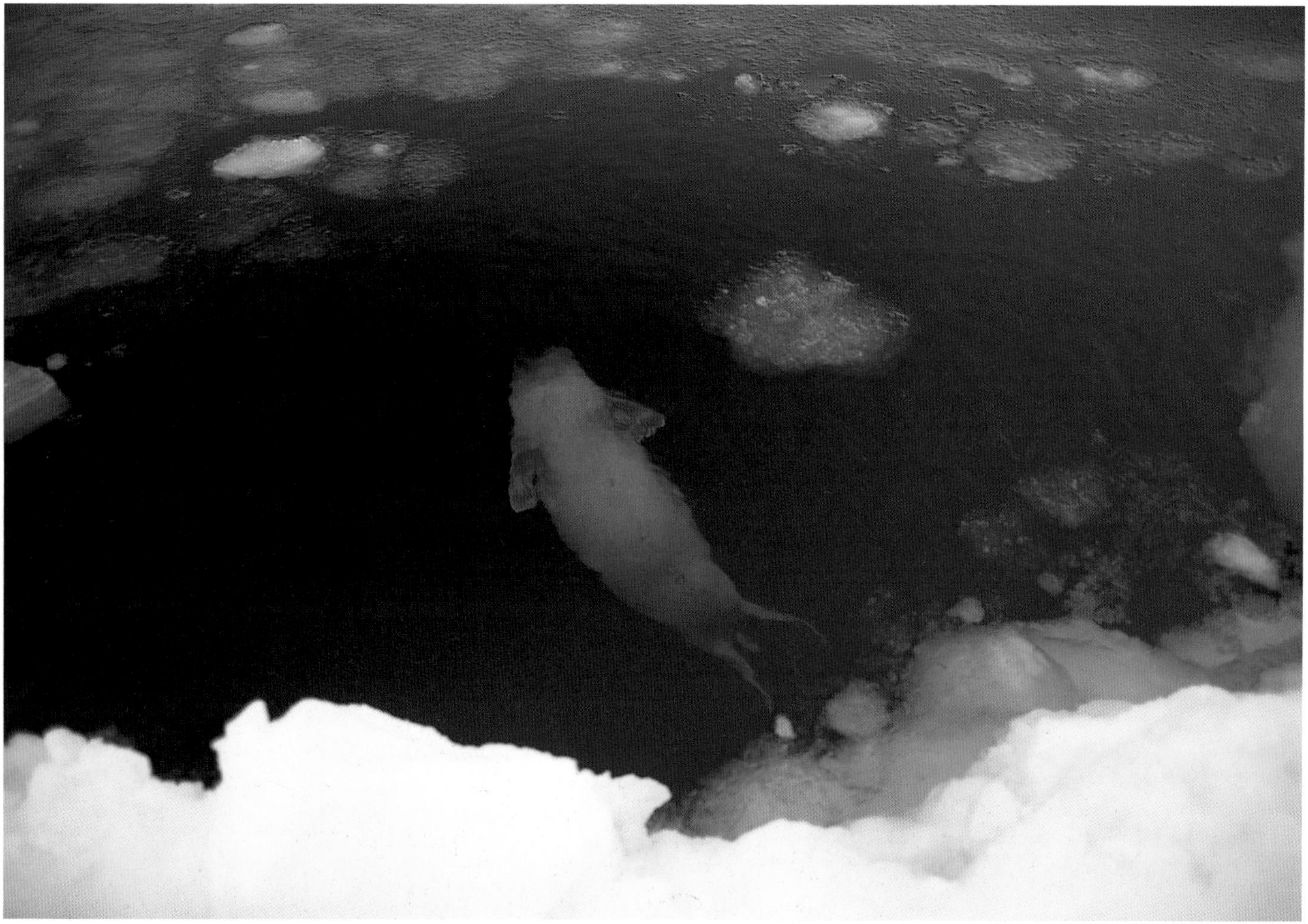

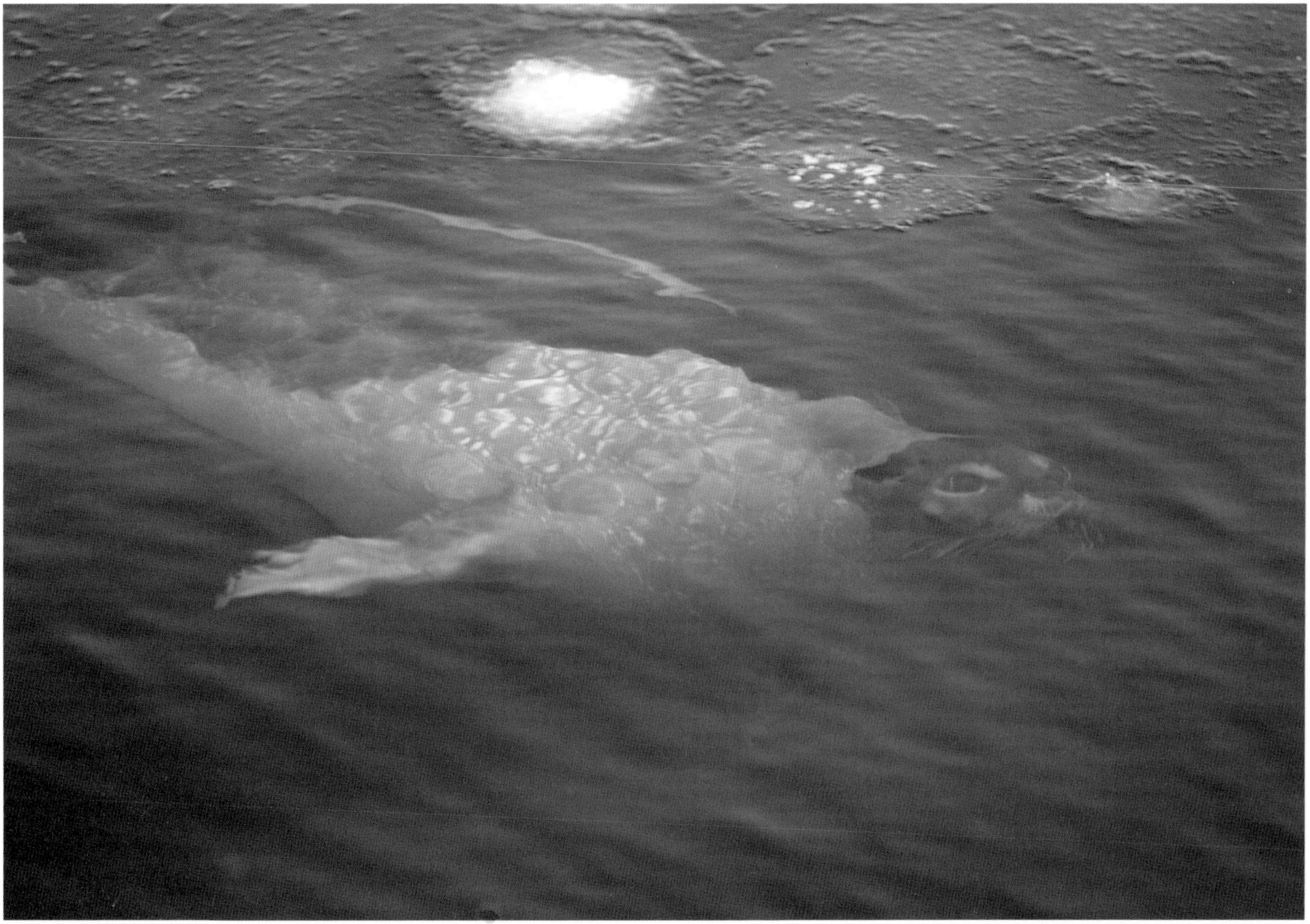

day eight

Approximately one week after birth, the pup becomes more agile. When the mother seal returns to the sea after nursing, the pup cries out and chases her. As it comes to the edge of the ice where its mother awaits, it approaches the water cautiously. Suddenly, the pup slips on the ice and falls into the sea. Stunned by the water, it paddles furiously, hitching itself back up onto the ice. This is how the pup learns to swim.

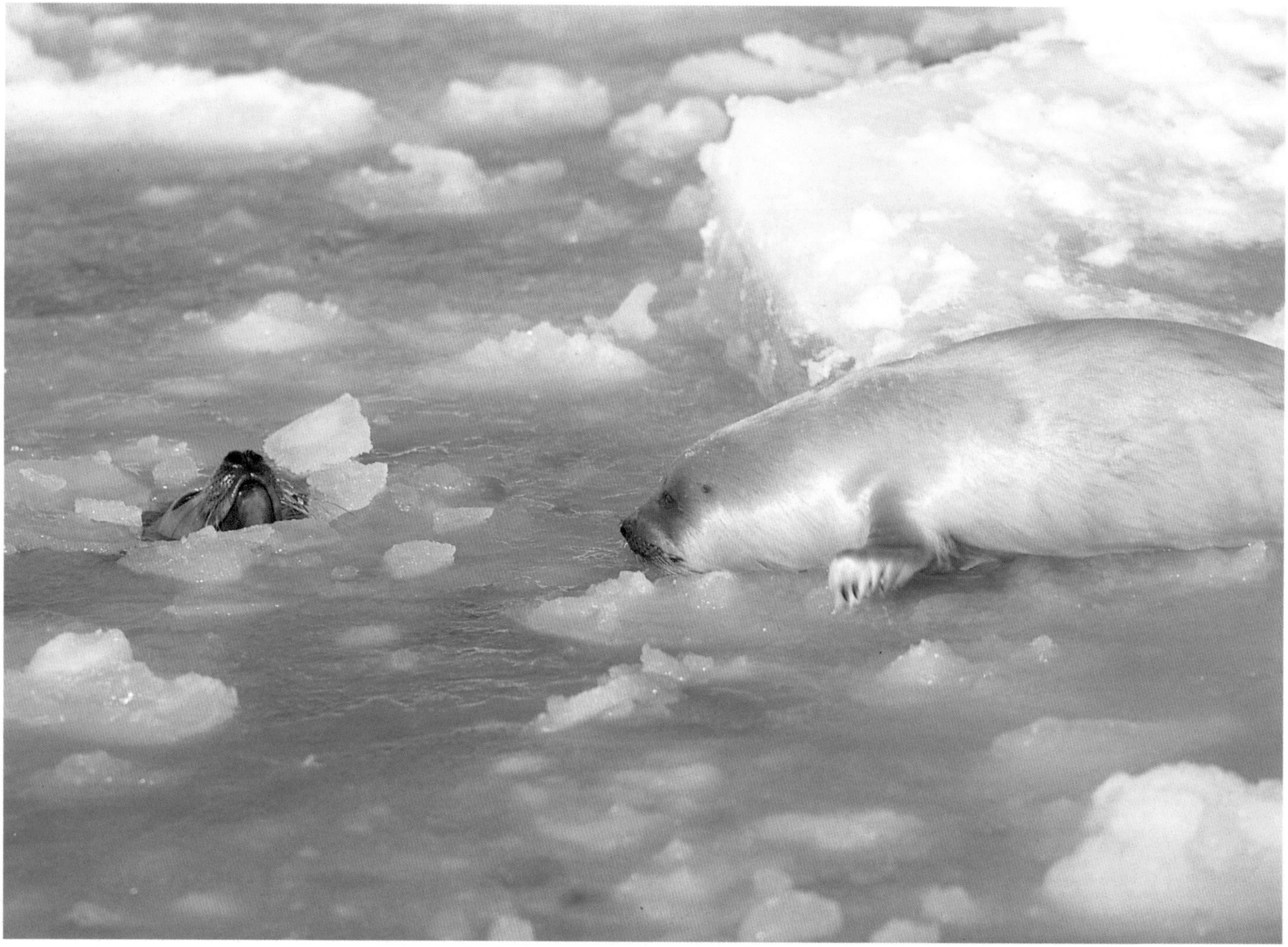

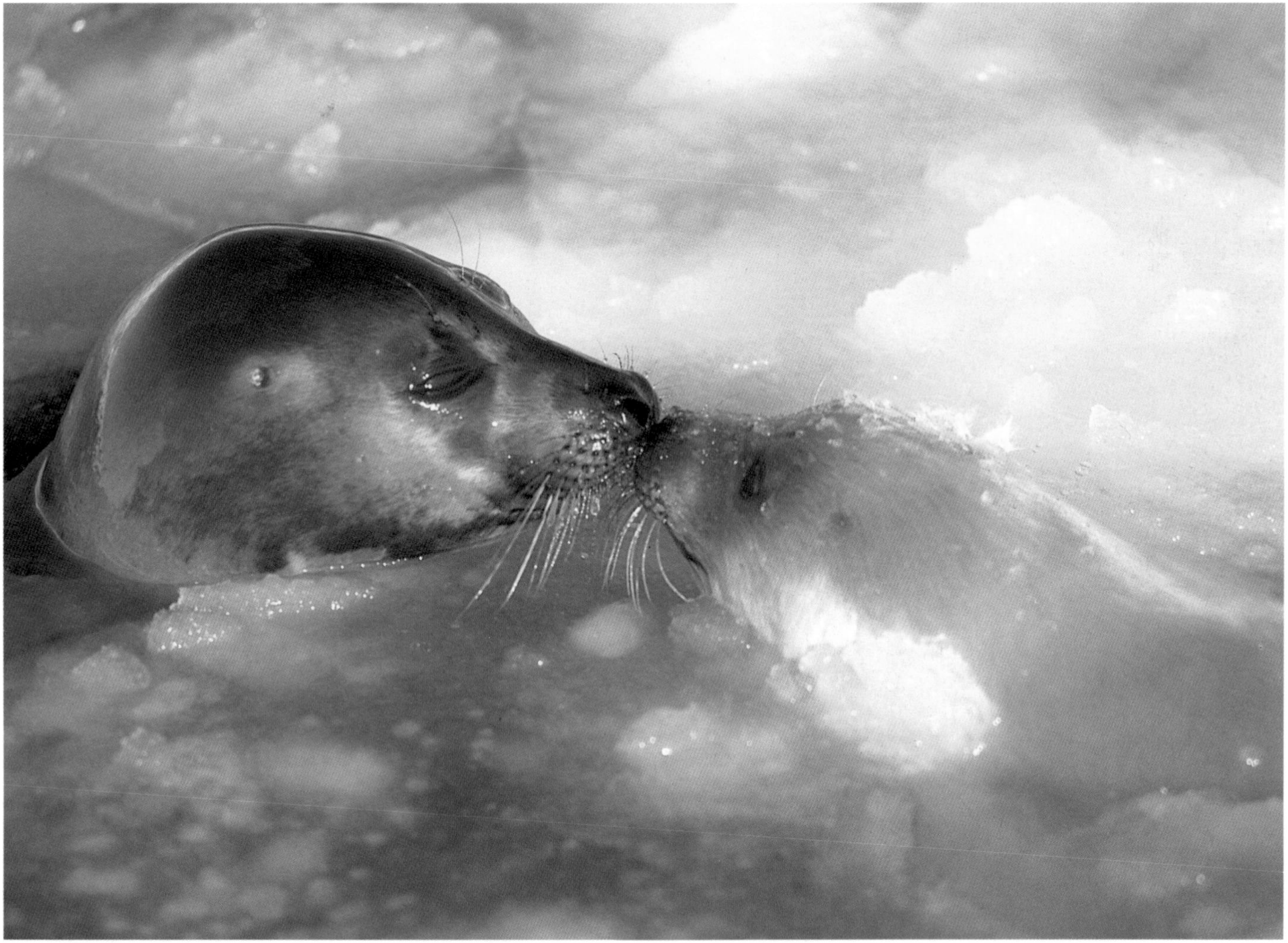

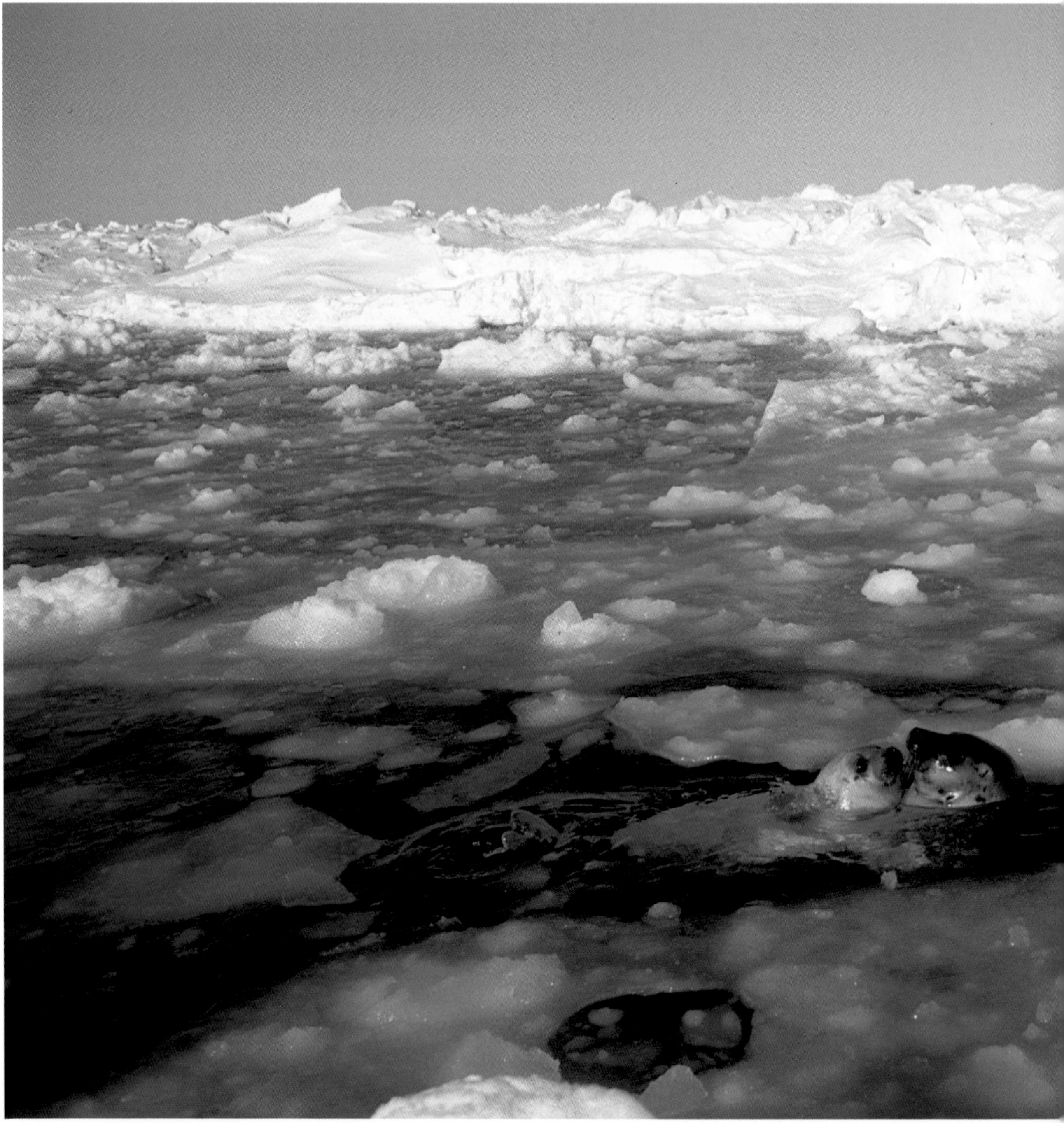

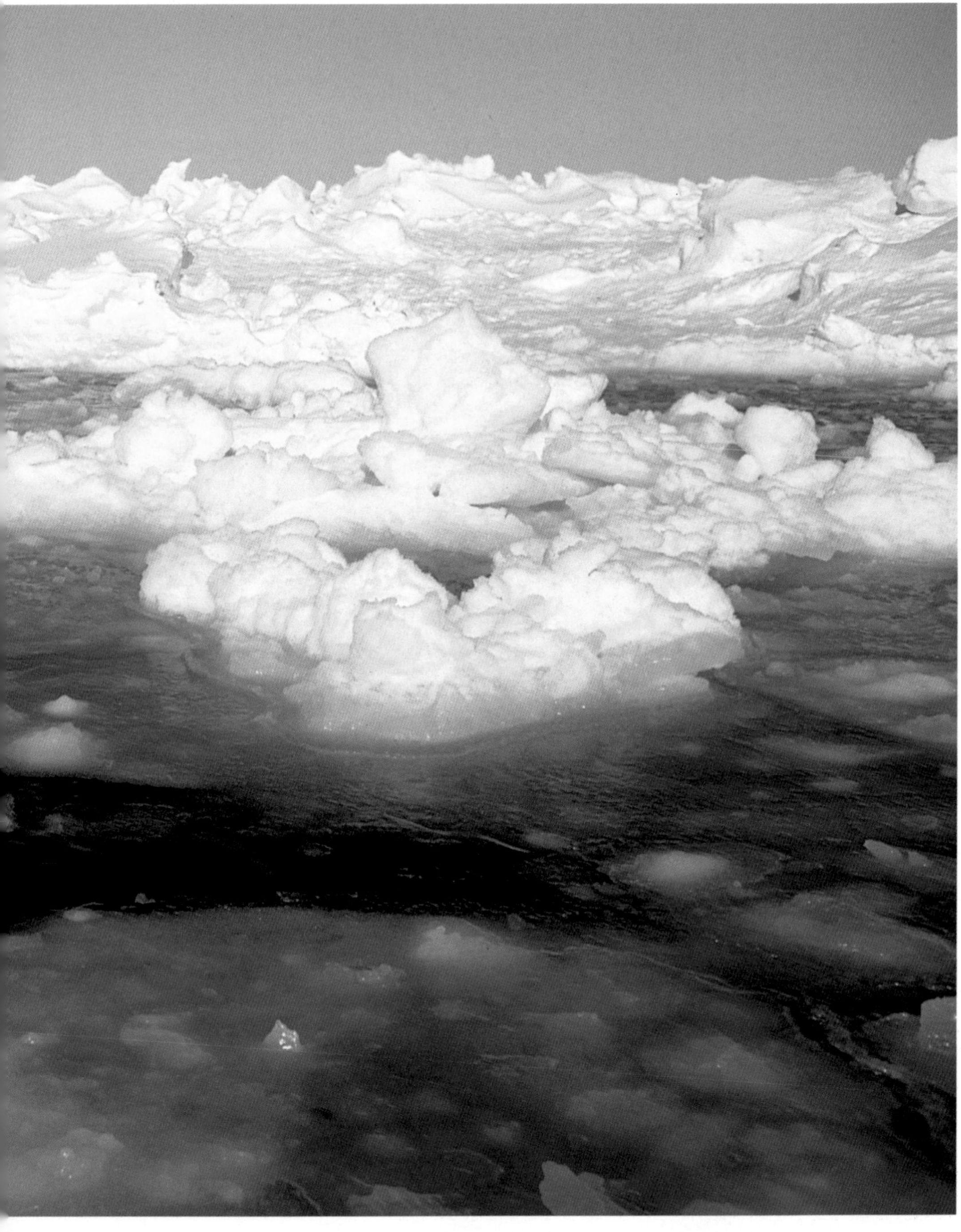

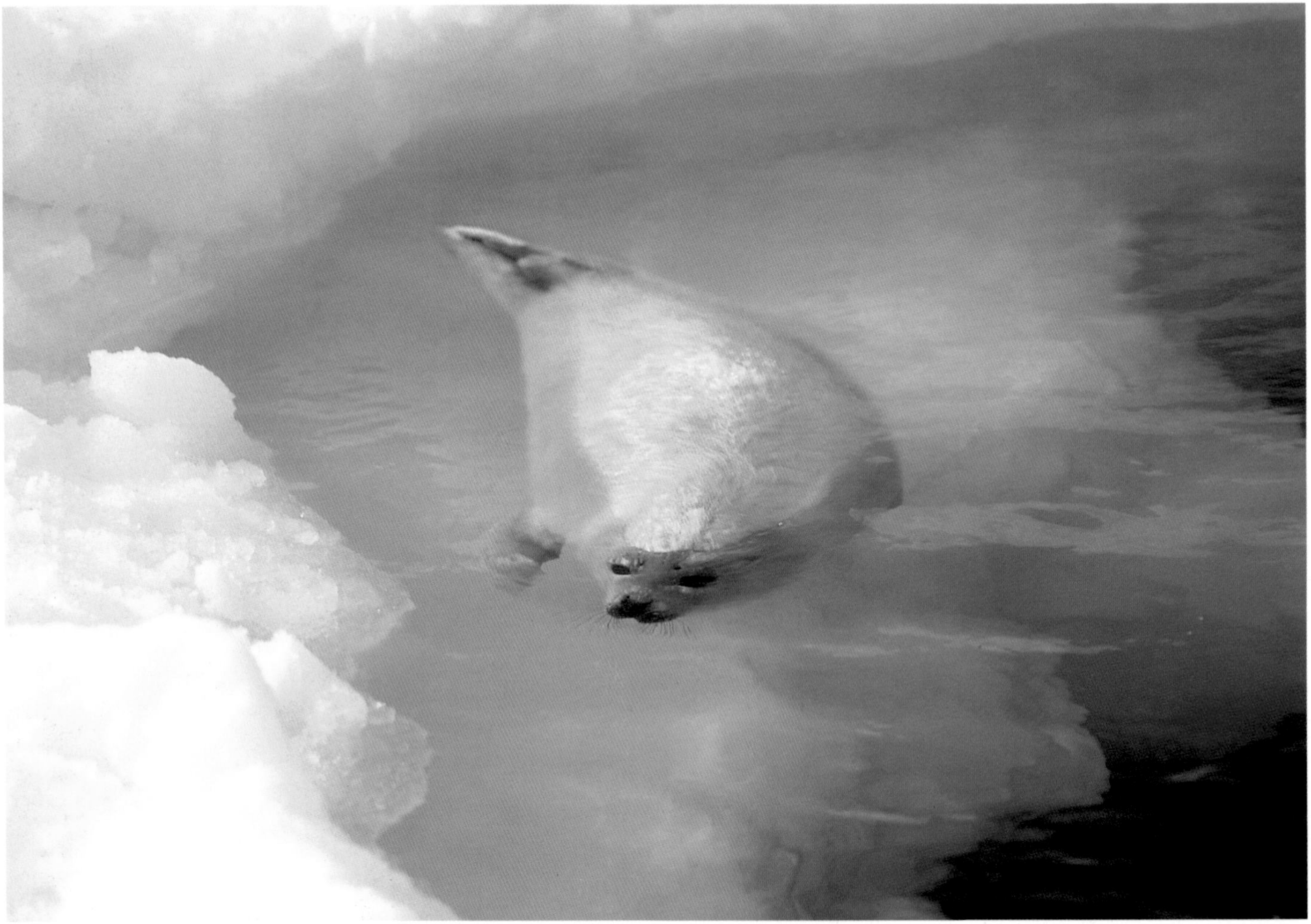

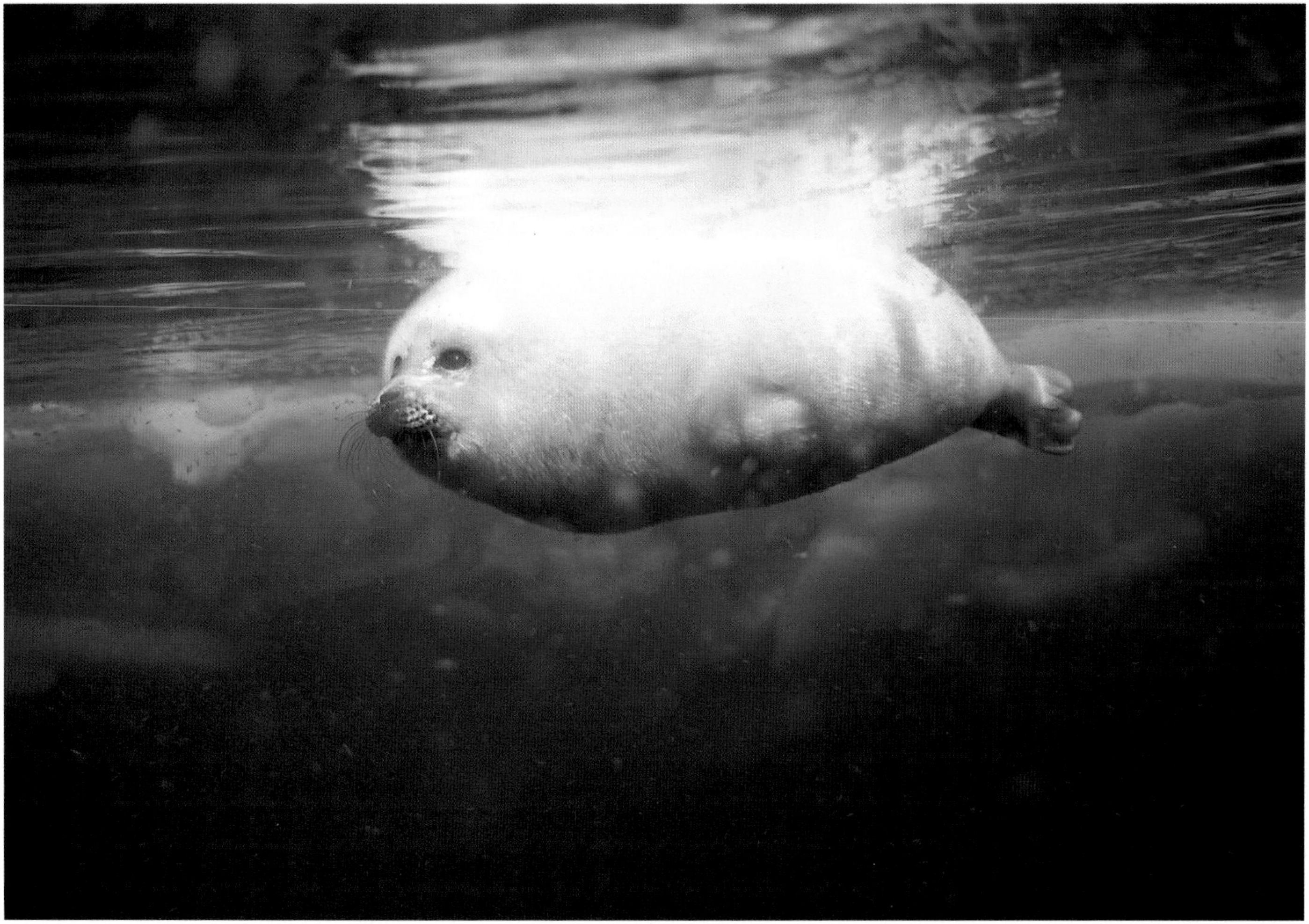

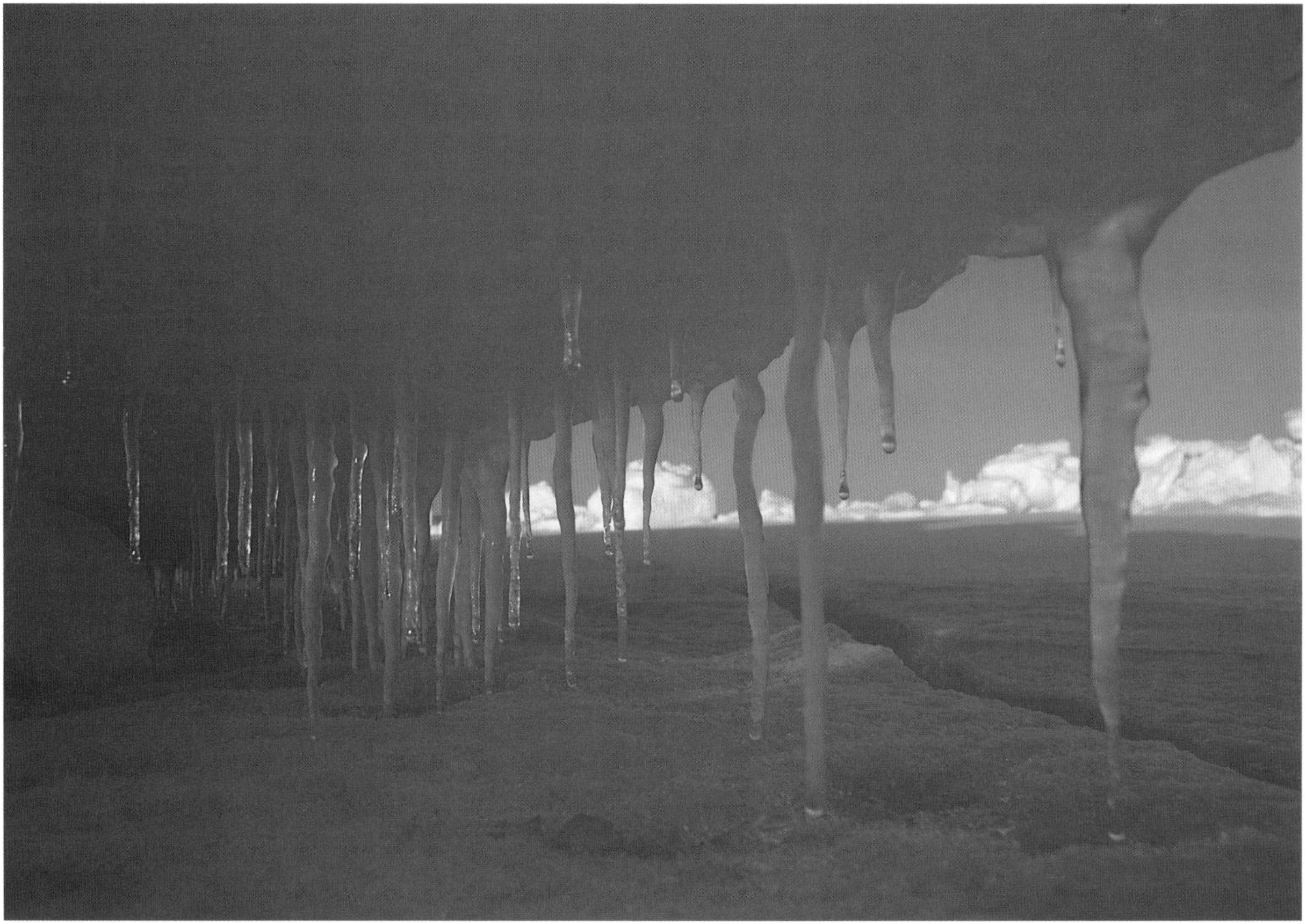

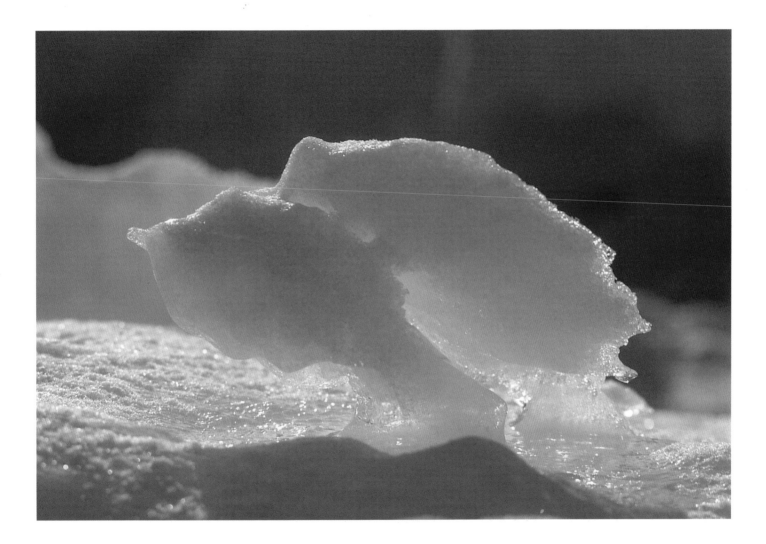

day nine

A storm suddenly approaches. Wind and snow blow furiously. With every step I take, my frozen footprint cracks immediately from the cold and blows away in shards, scraping against the ice. As the wind howls and icicles form on my eyebrows, I shade my eyes with my hand against the snow blowing into my face—and suddenly two round eyes appear, buried in this white landscape.

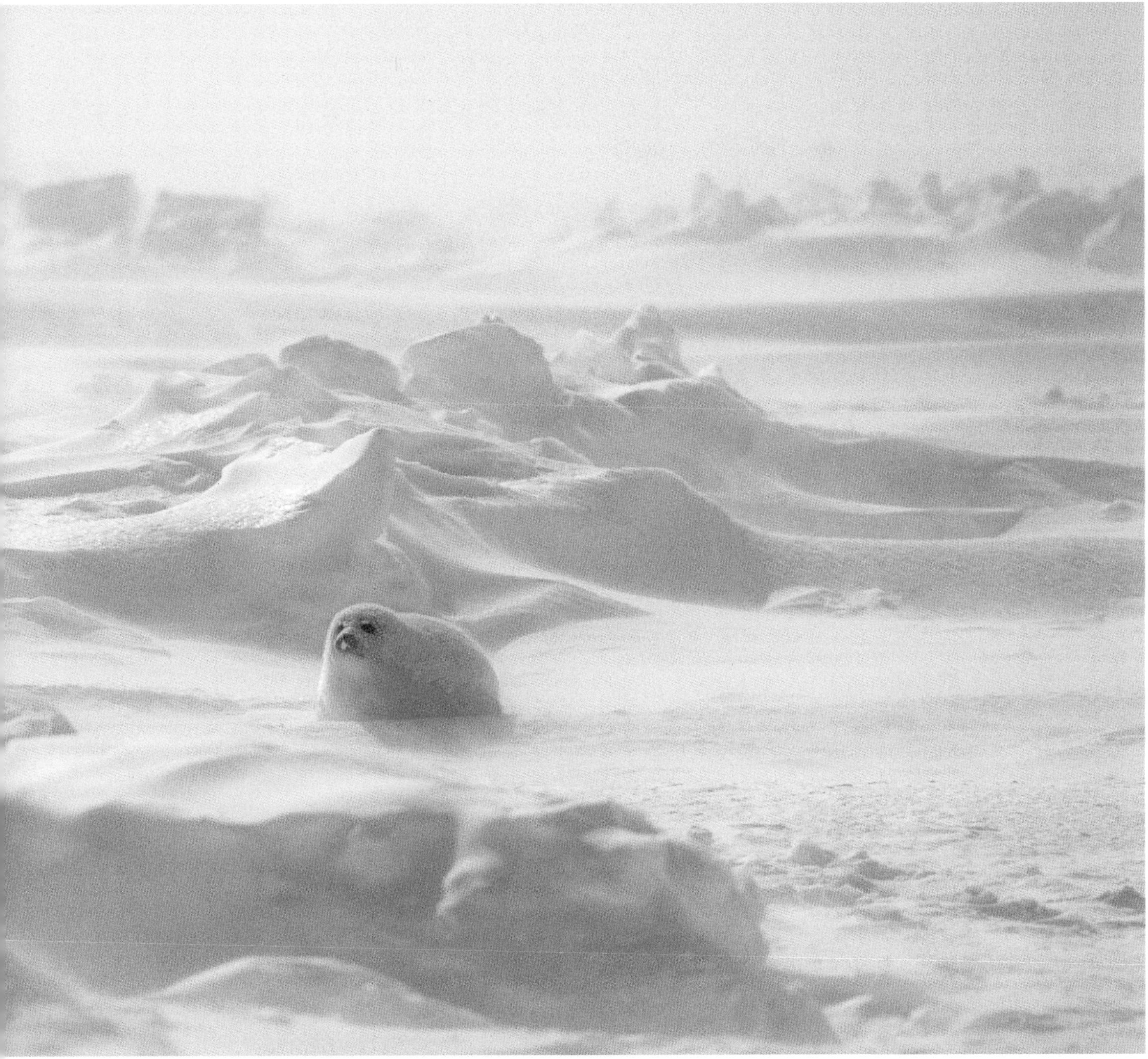

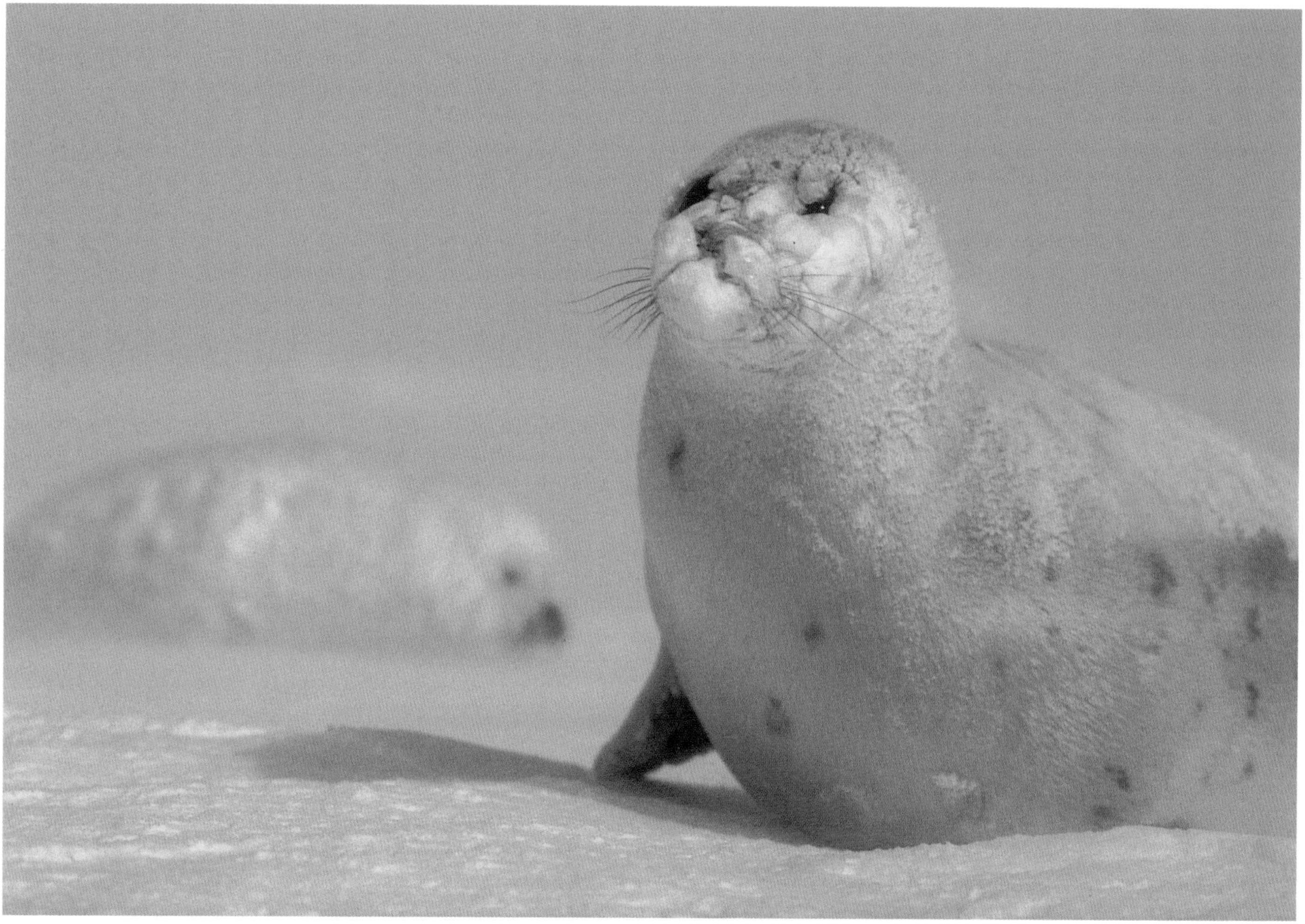

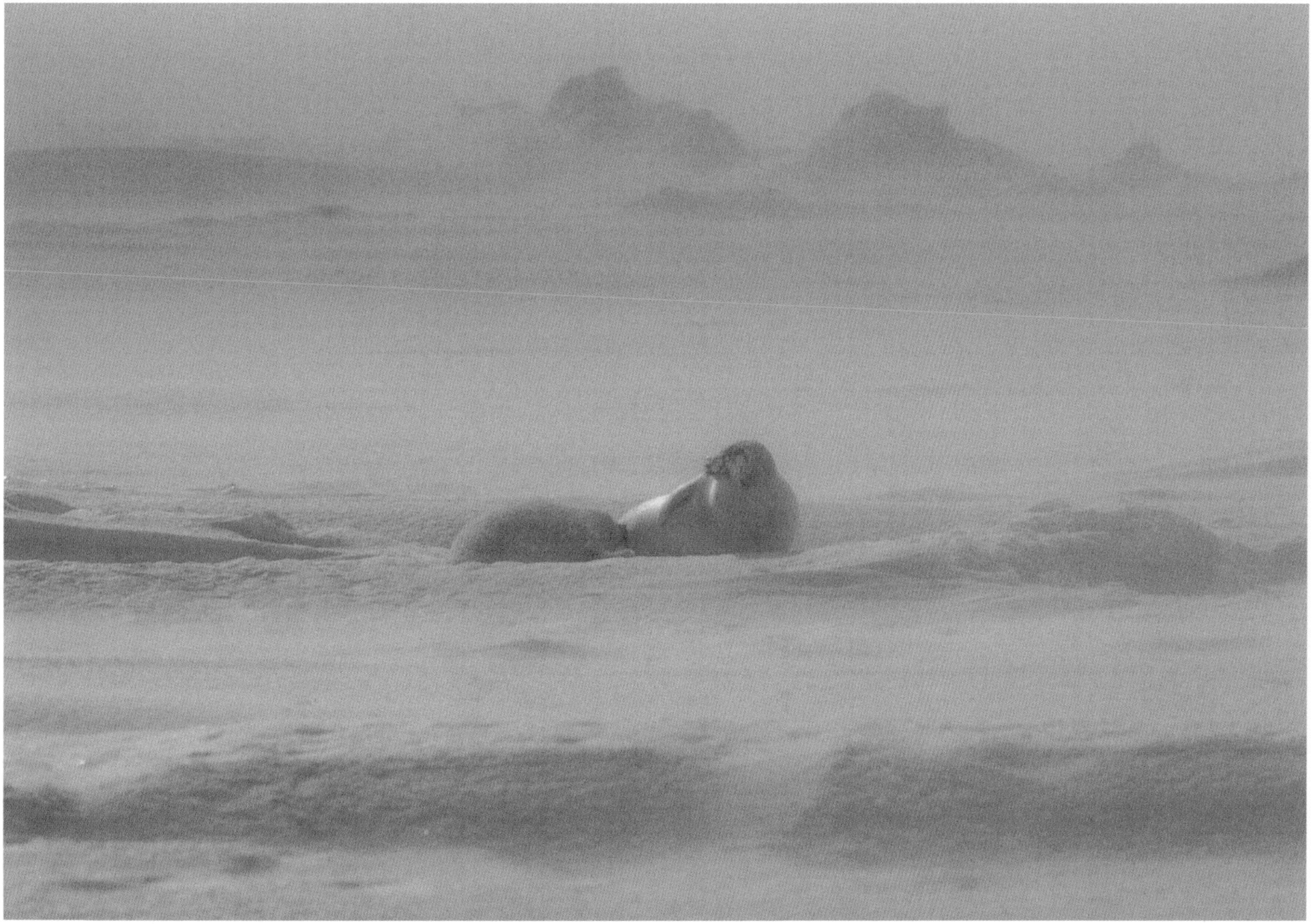

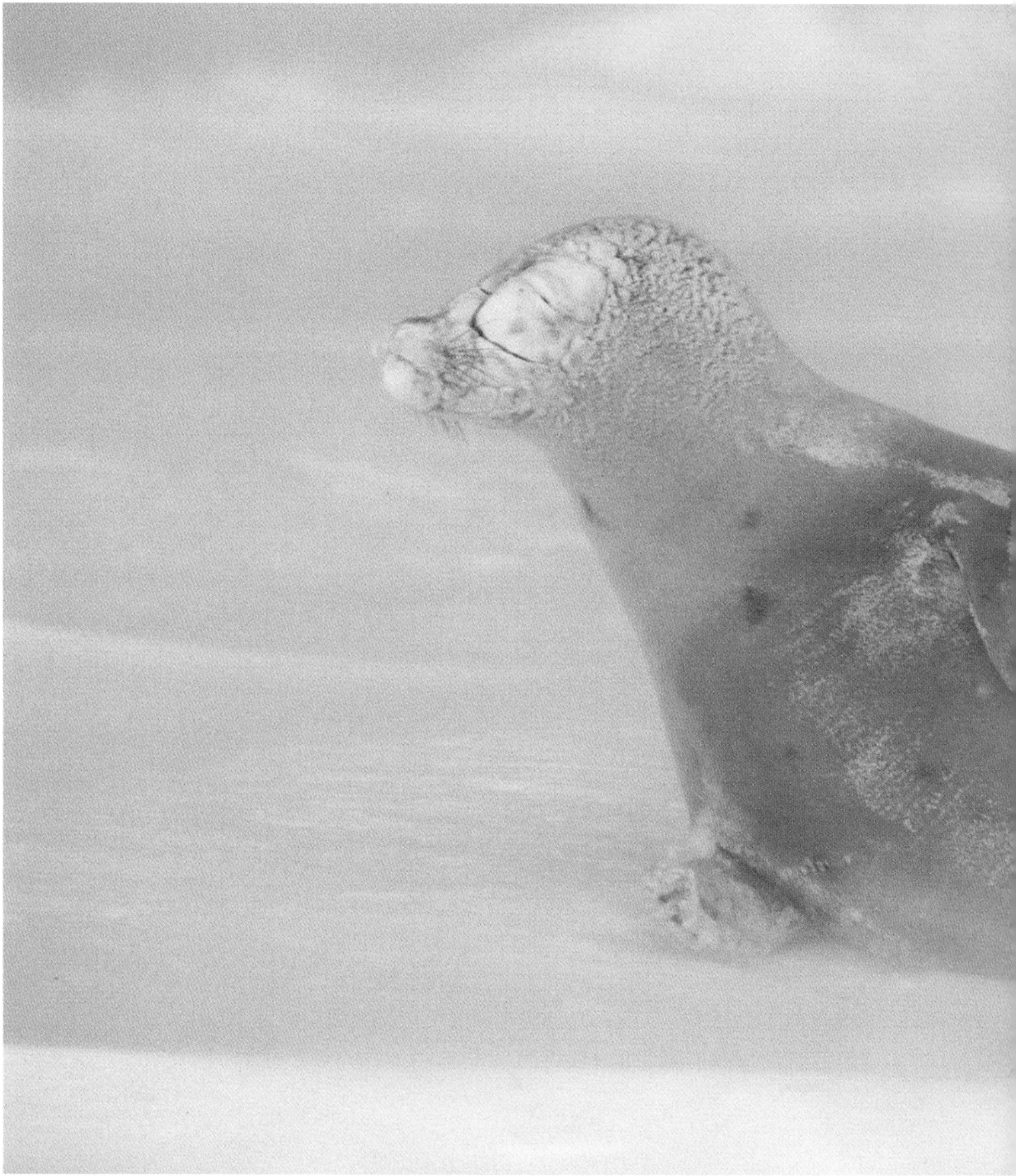

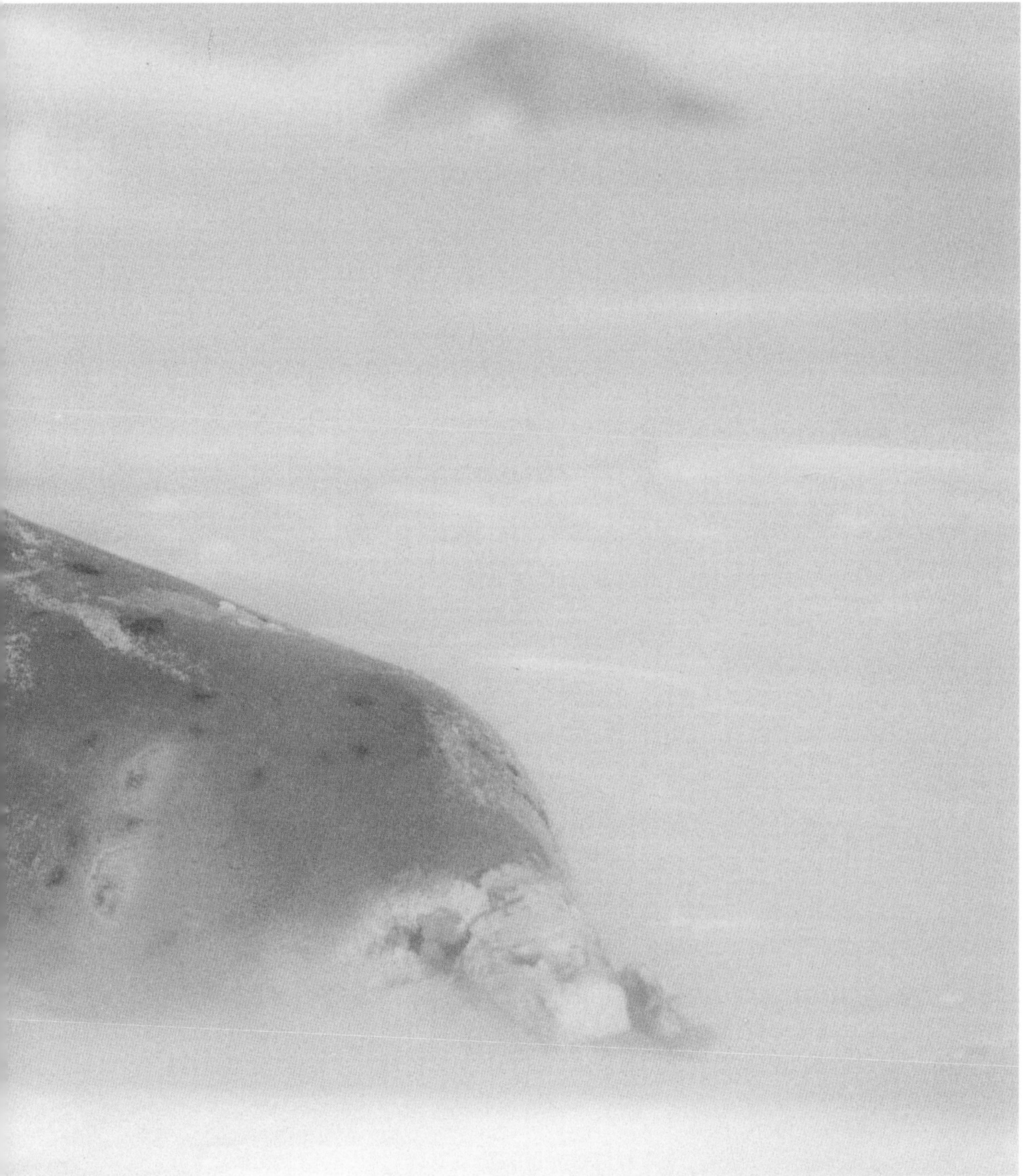

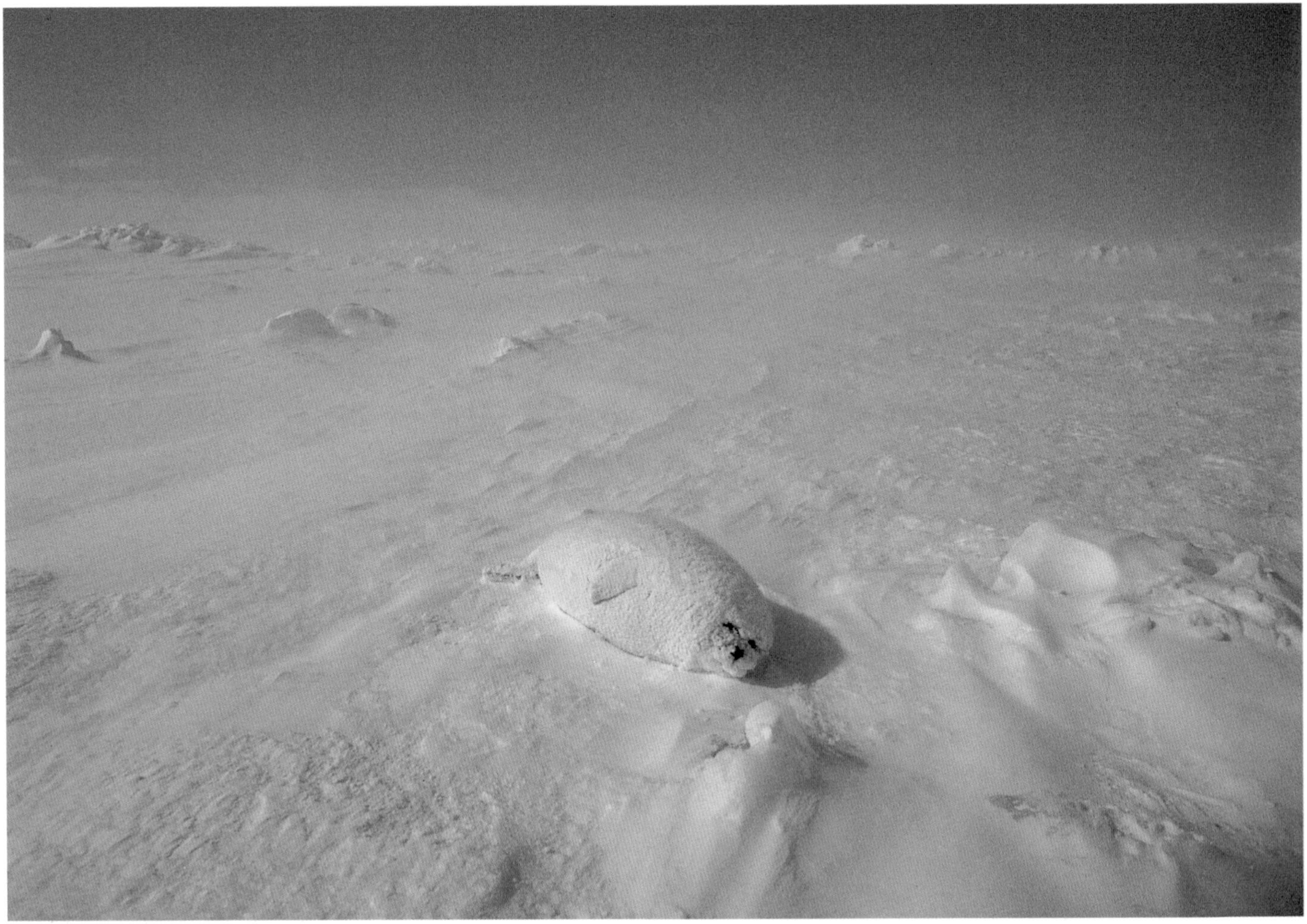

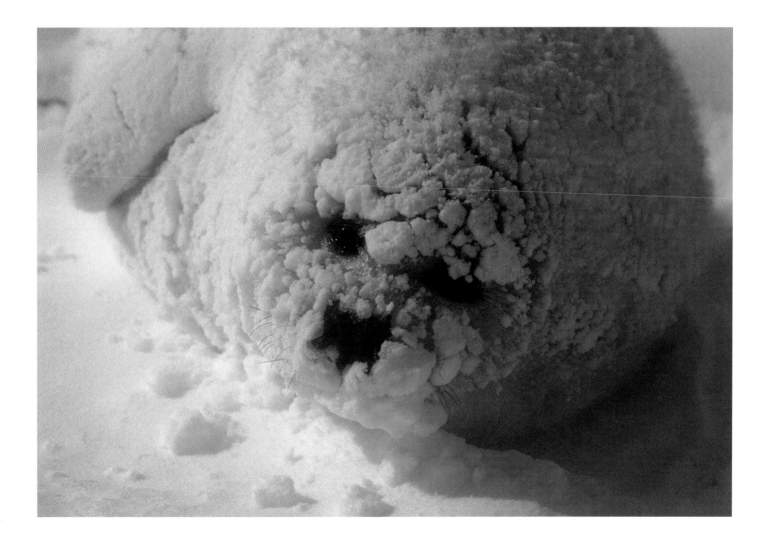

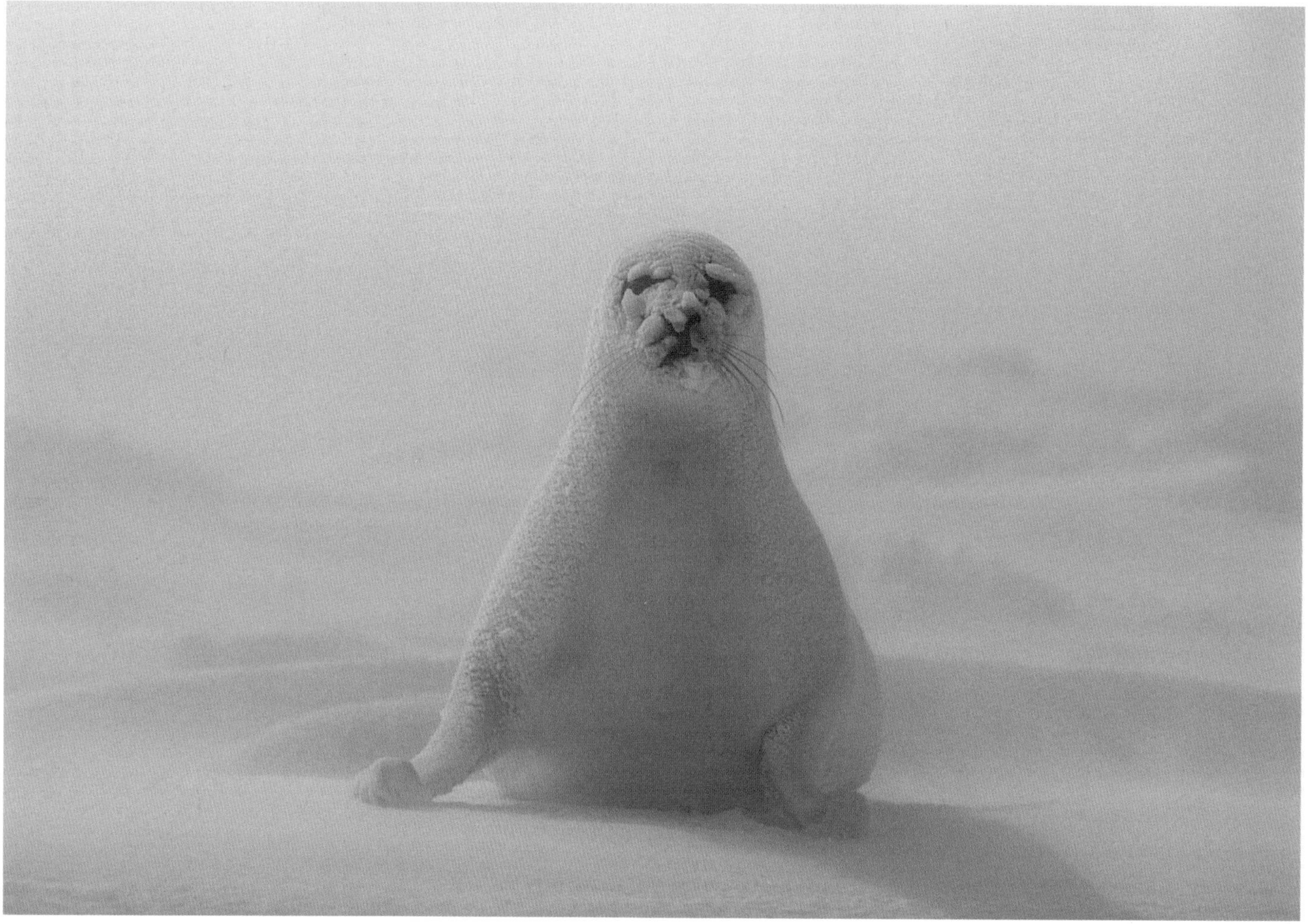

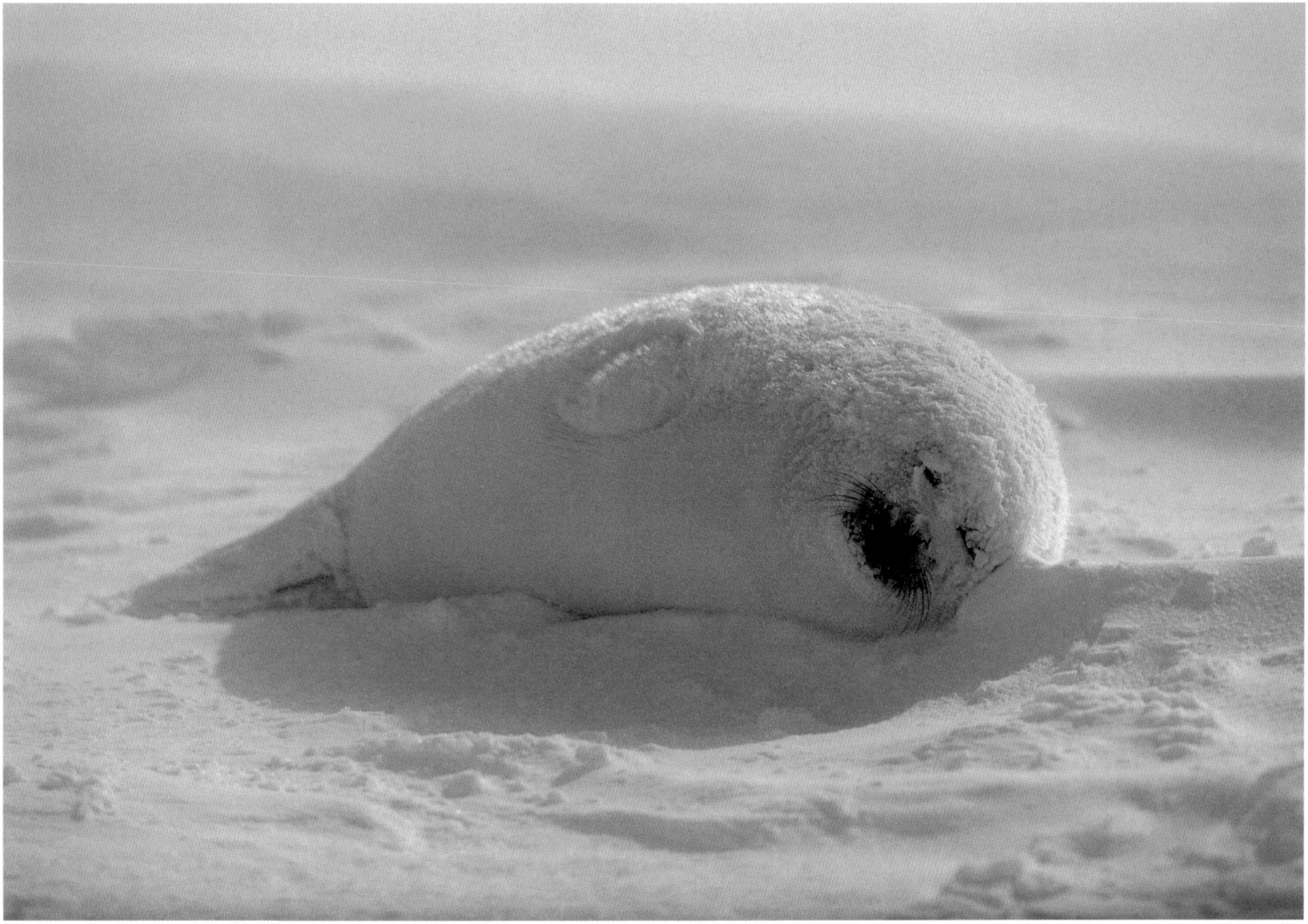

day ten

The following morning, after the storm, the sun is blinding. Light reflected by the ice and the dry, blowing wind makes my eyes water. Both human and seal eyes tear for protection. When the wind dies down, the tears stop flowing, and the ten-day-old pup is overjoyed. Round and fat, both the small seals and the big seals begin to look carefree as they gradually forget their worries.

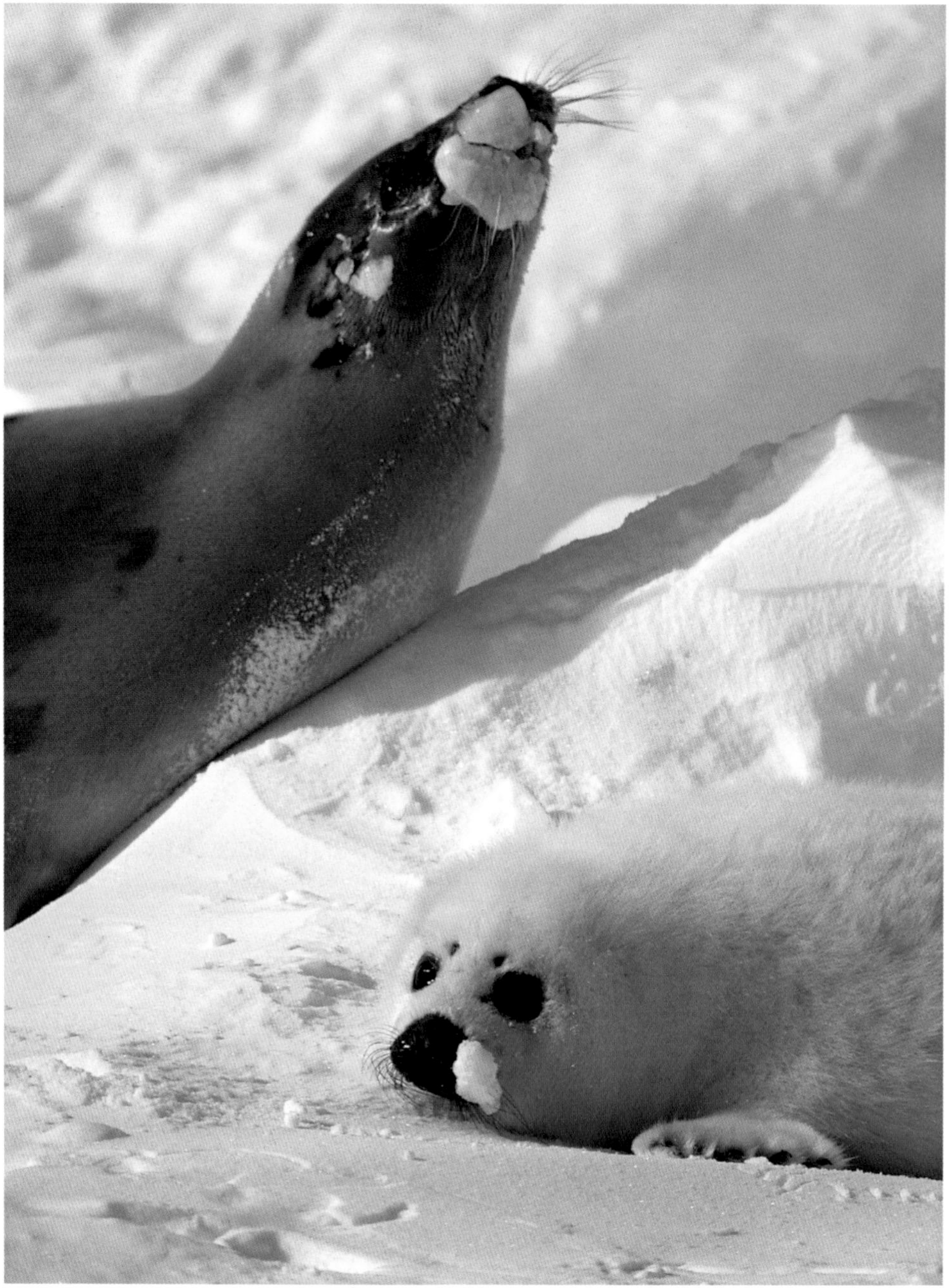

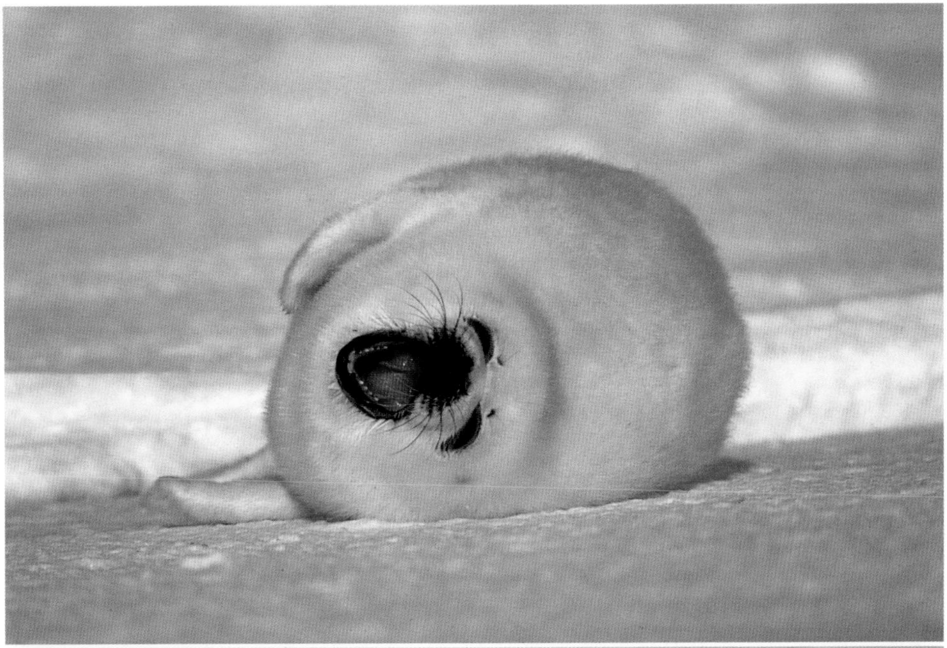

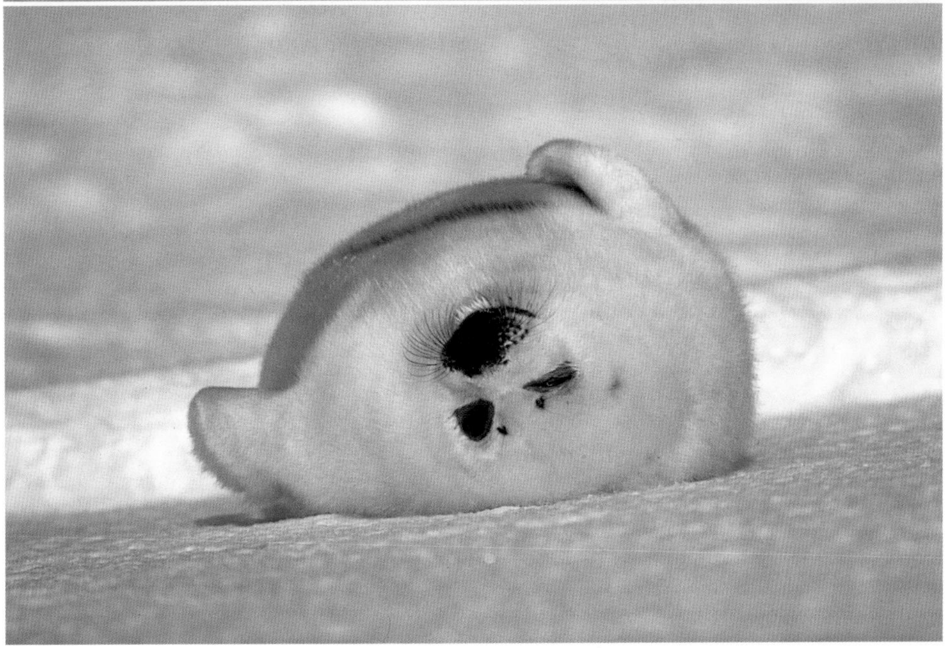

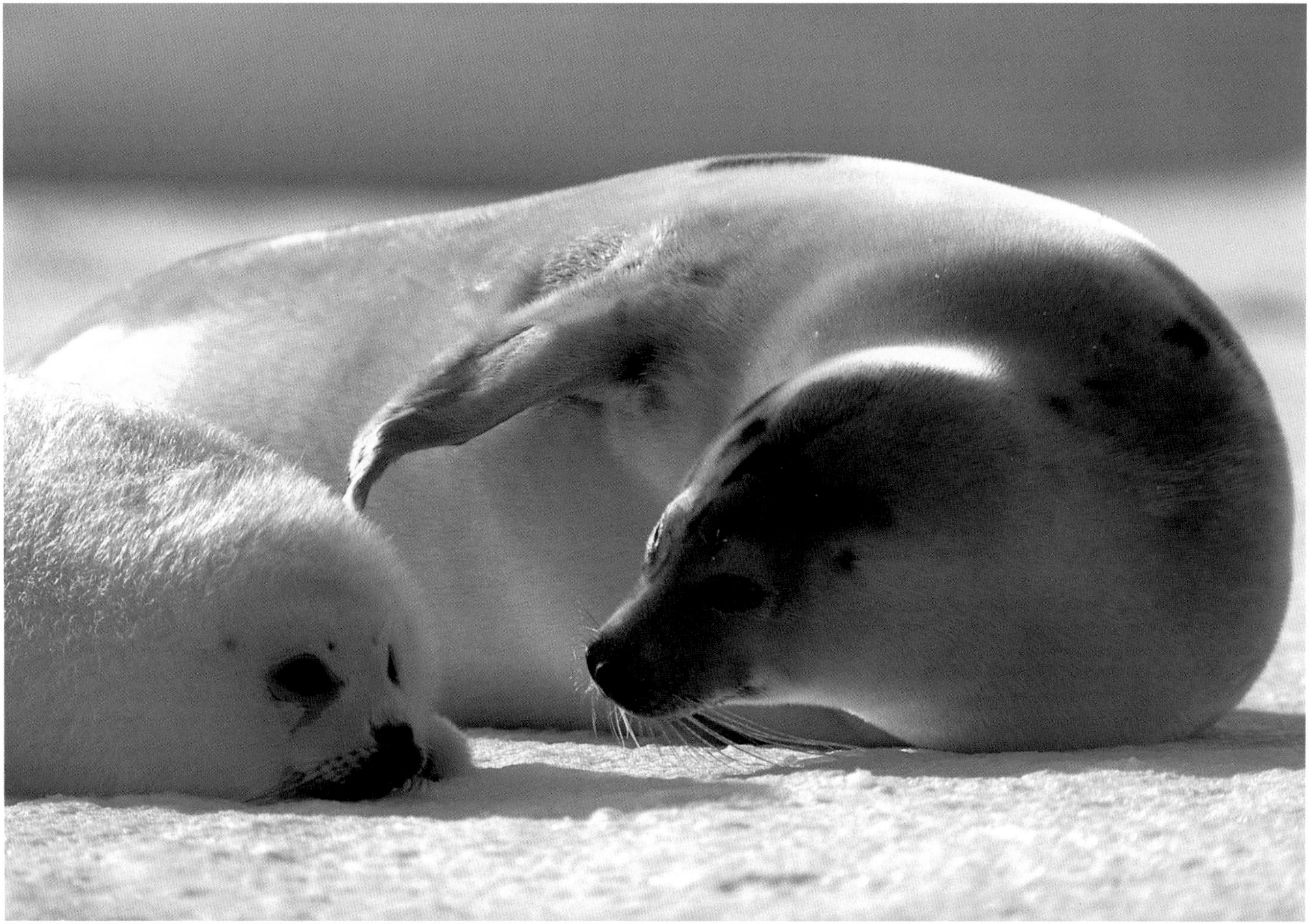

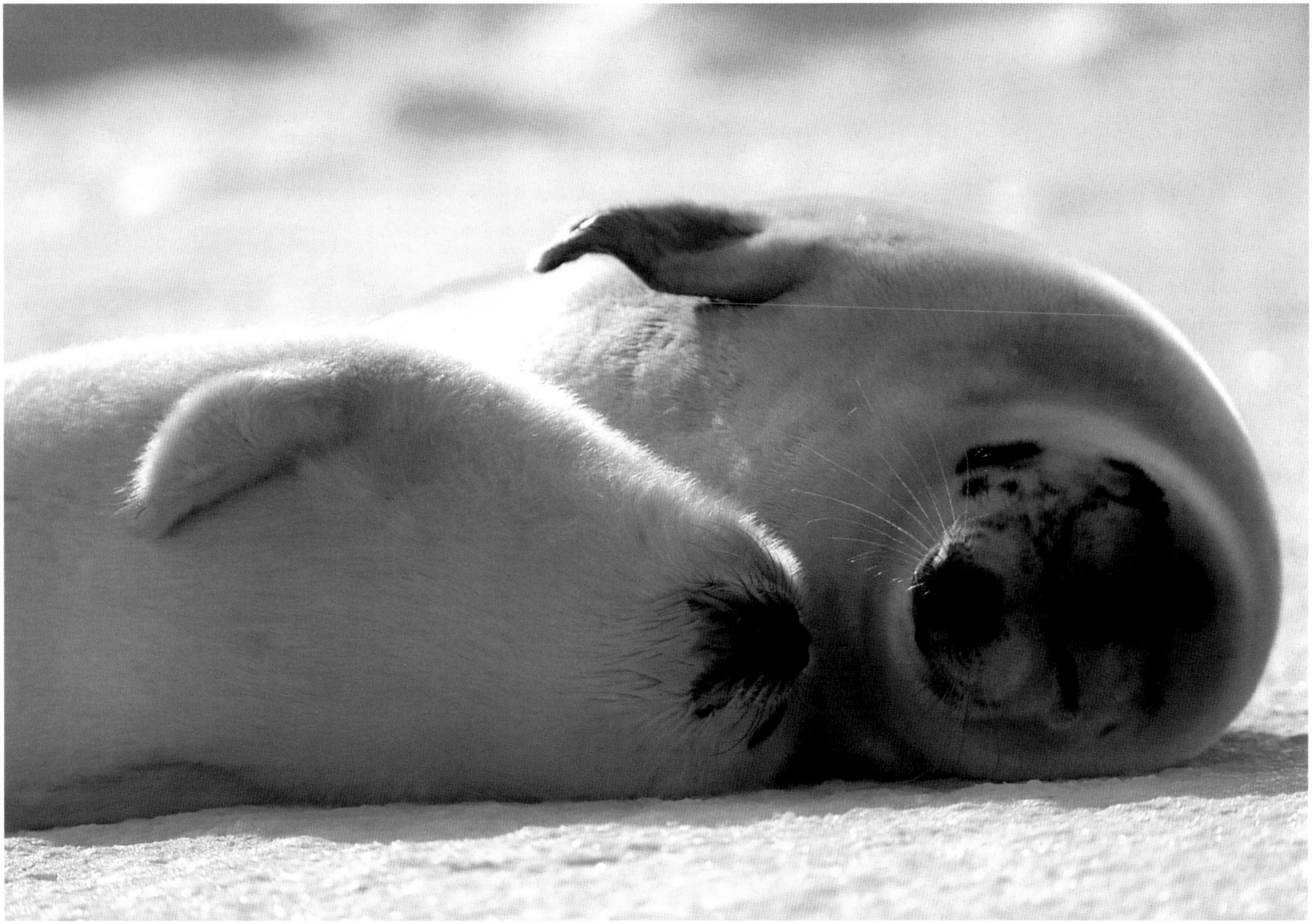

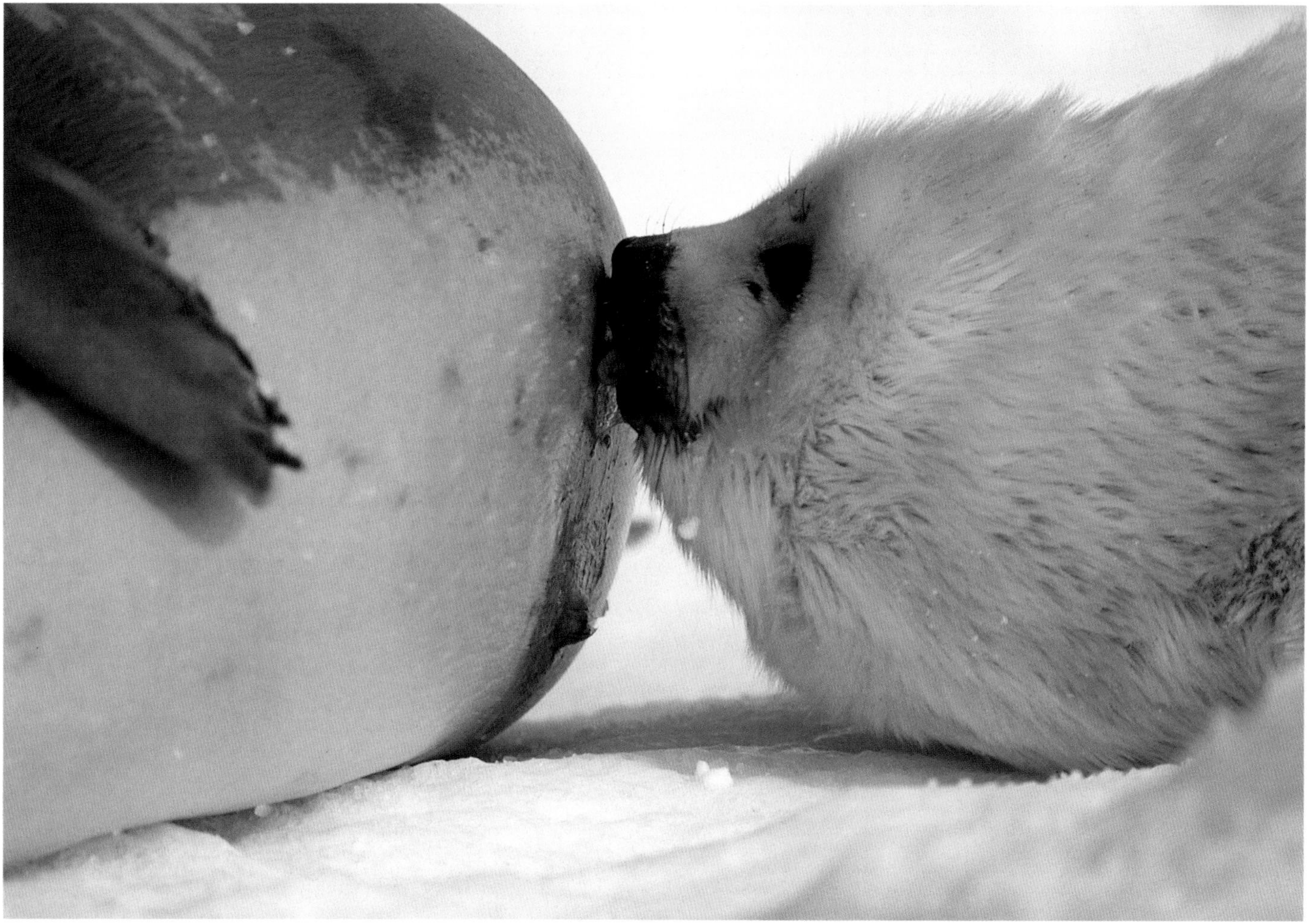

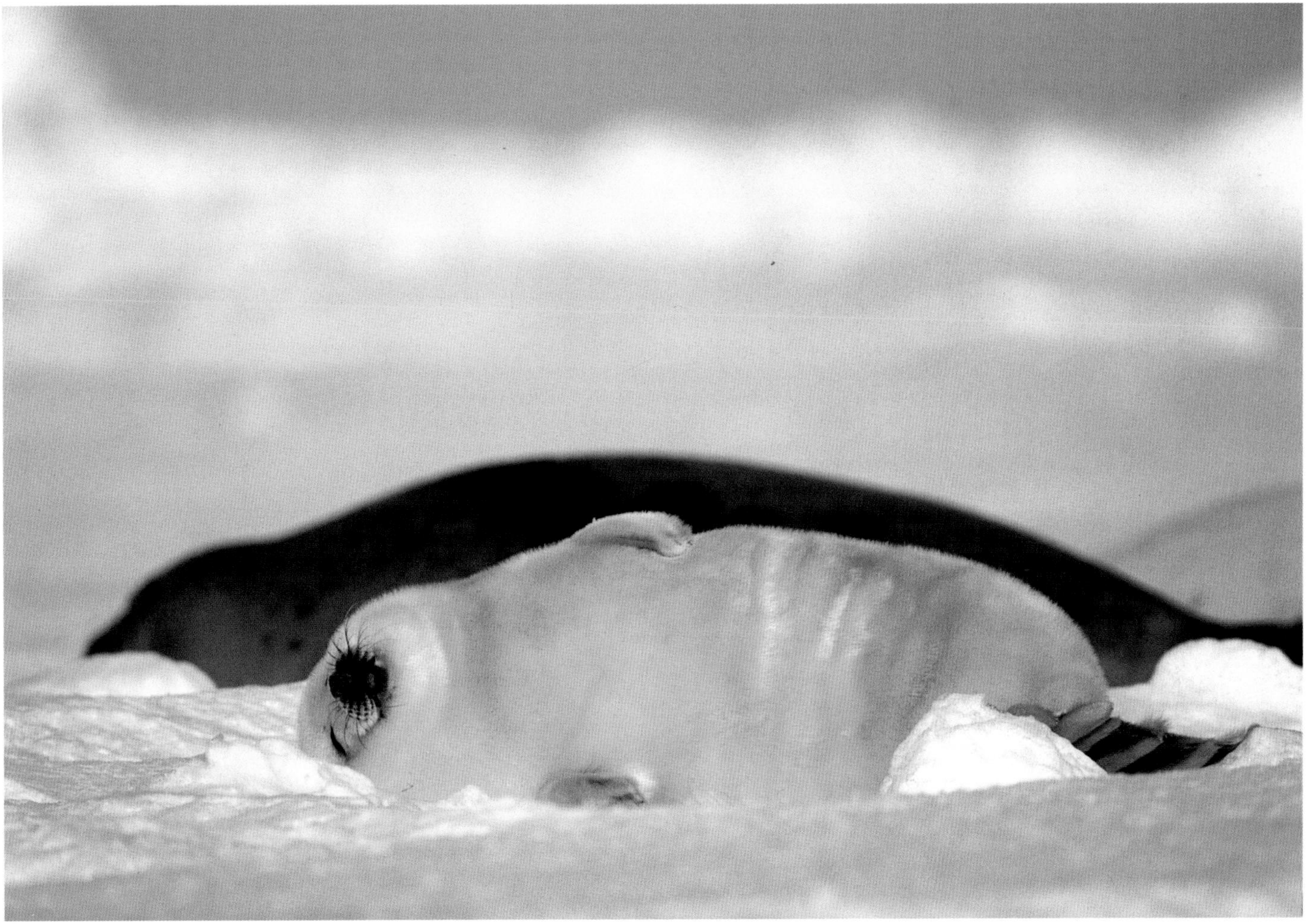

day eleven

The clear days continue and the winds are less harsh. The ice splits, opening up to the sea. Nursing decreases rapidly. The mother seal appears less and less frequently, gradually disappearing from the ice plains. After mating, she swims freely in the sea, several hundred yards deep. The white pup cries to be fed, but the mother seal does not respond.

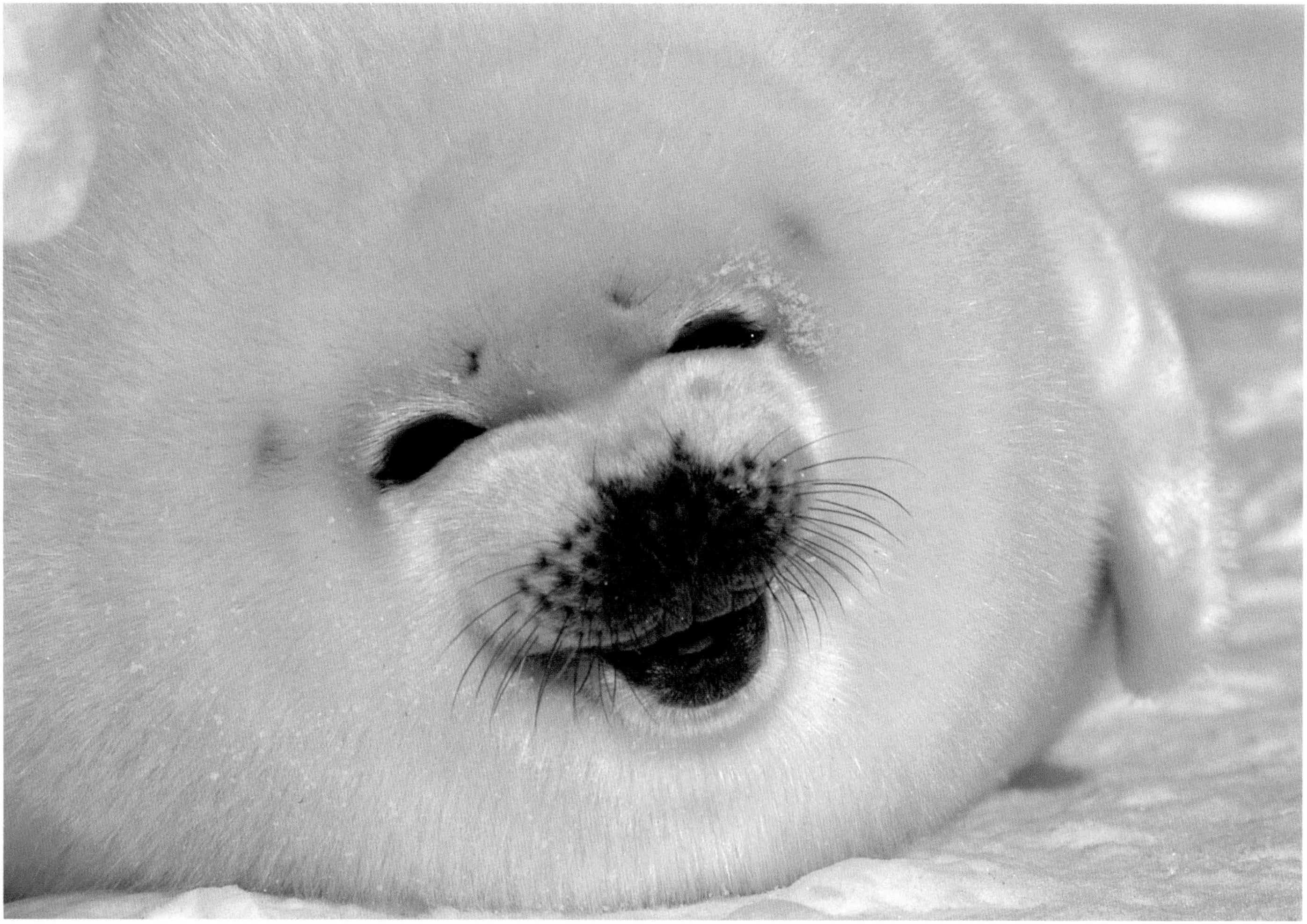

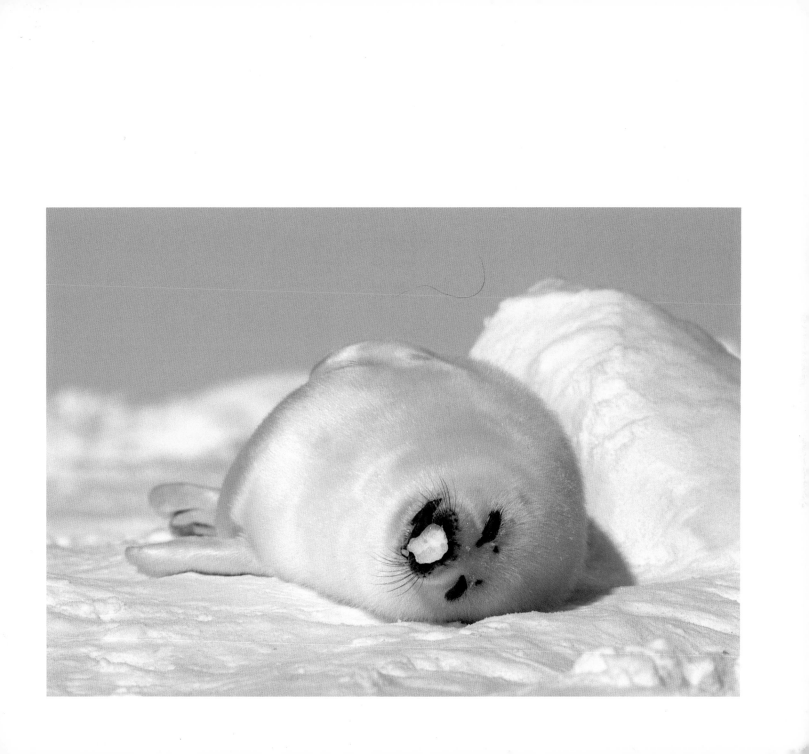

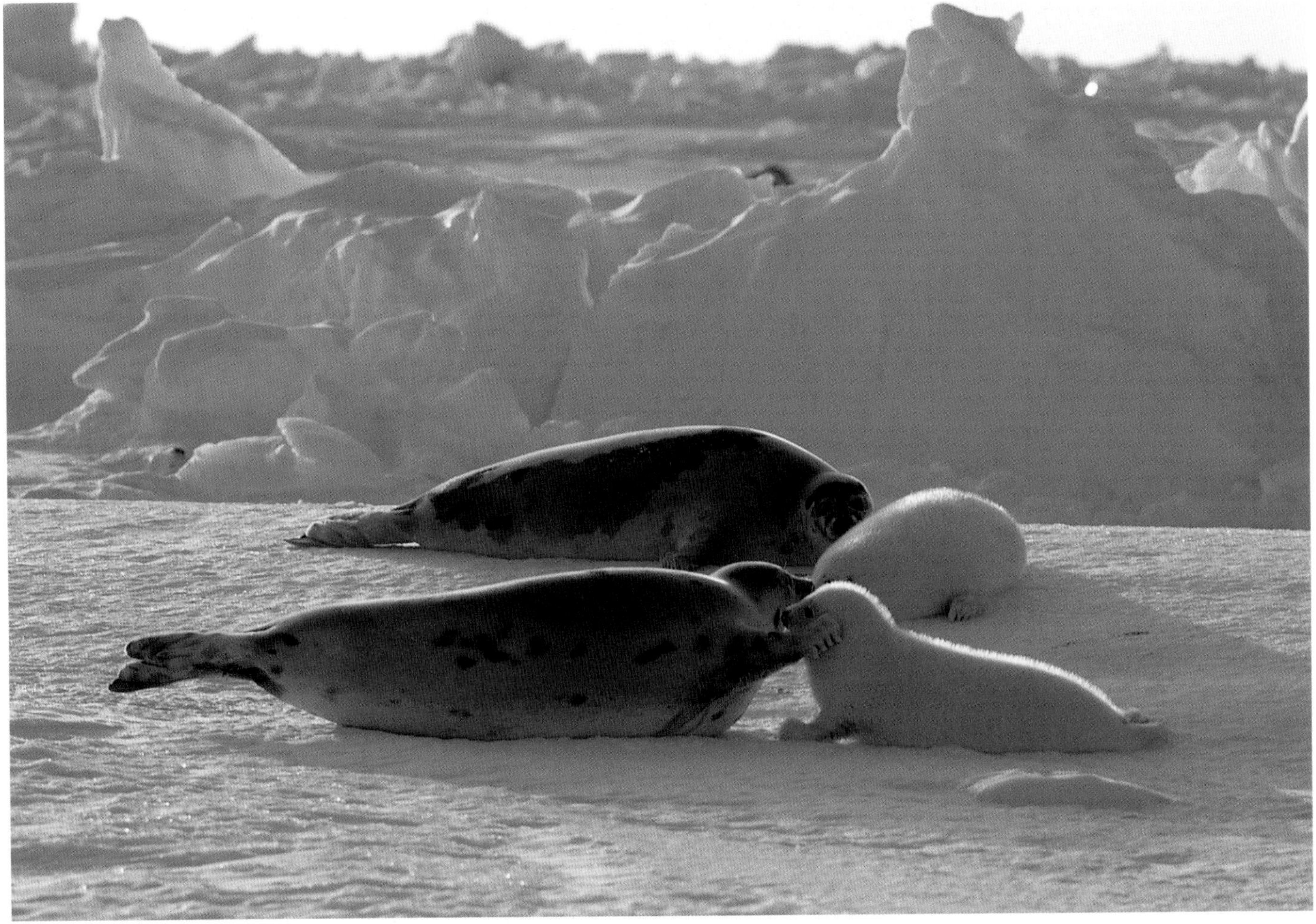

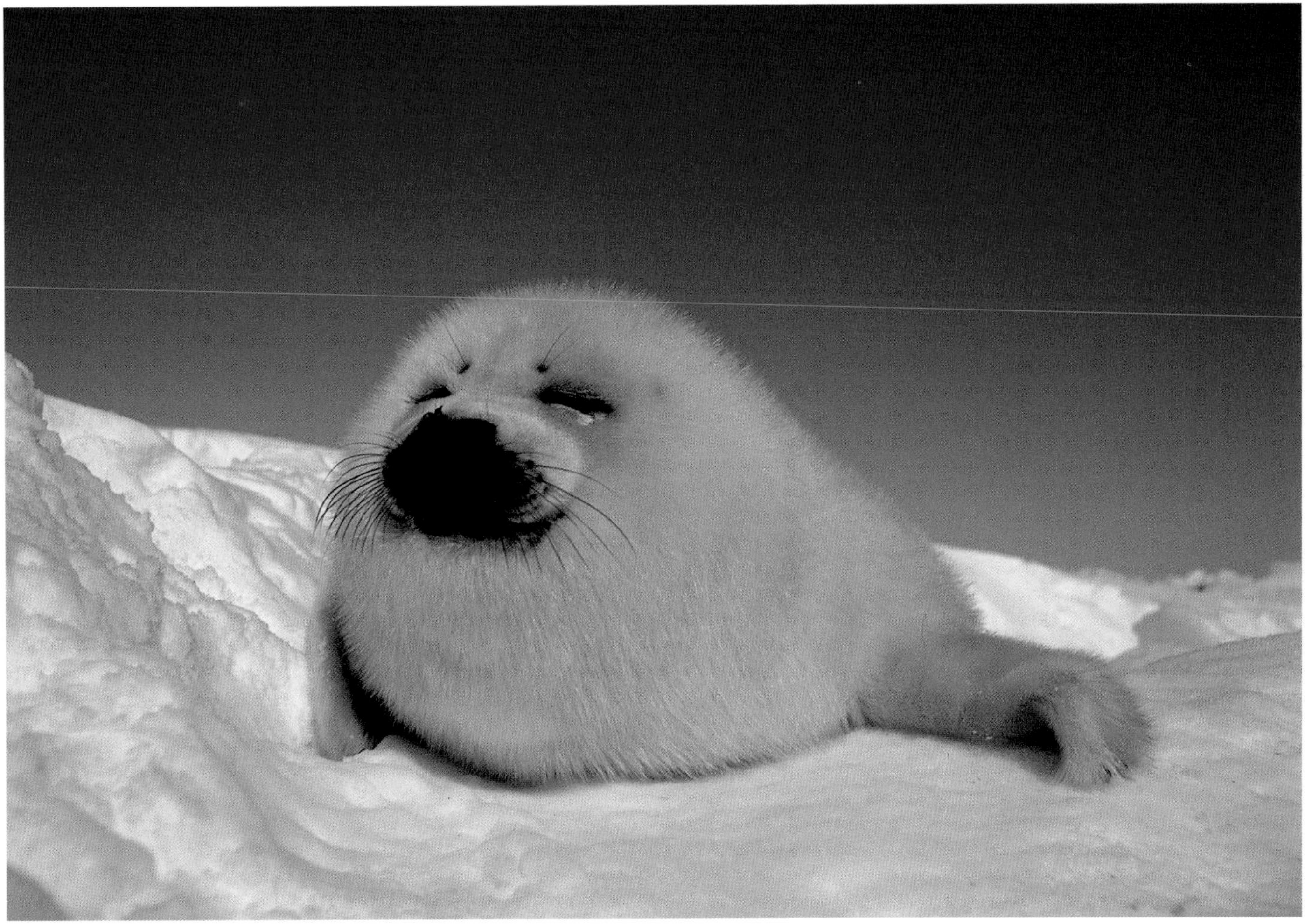

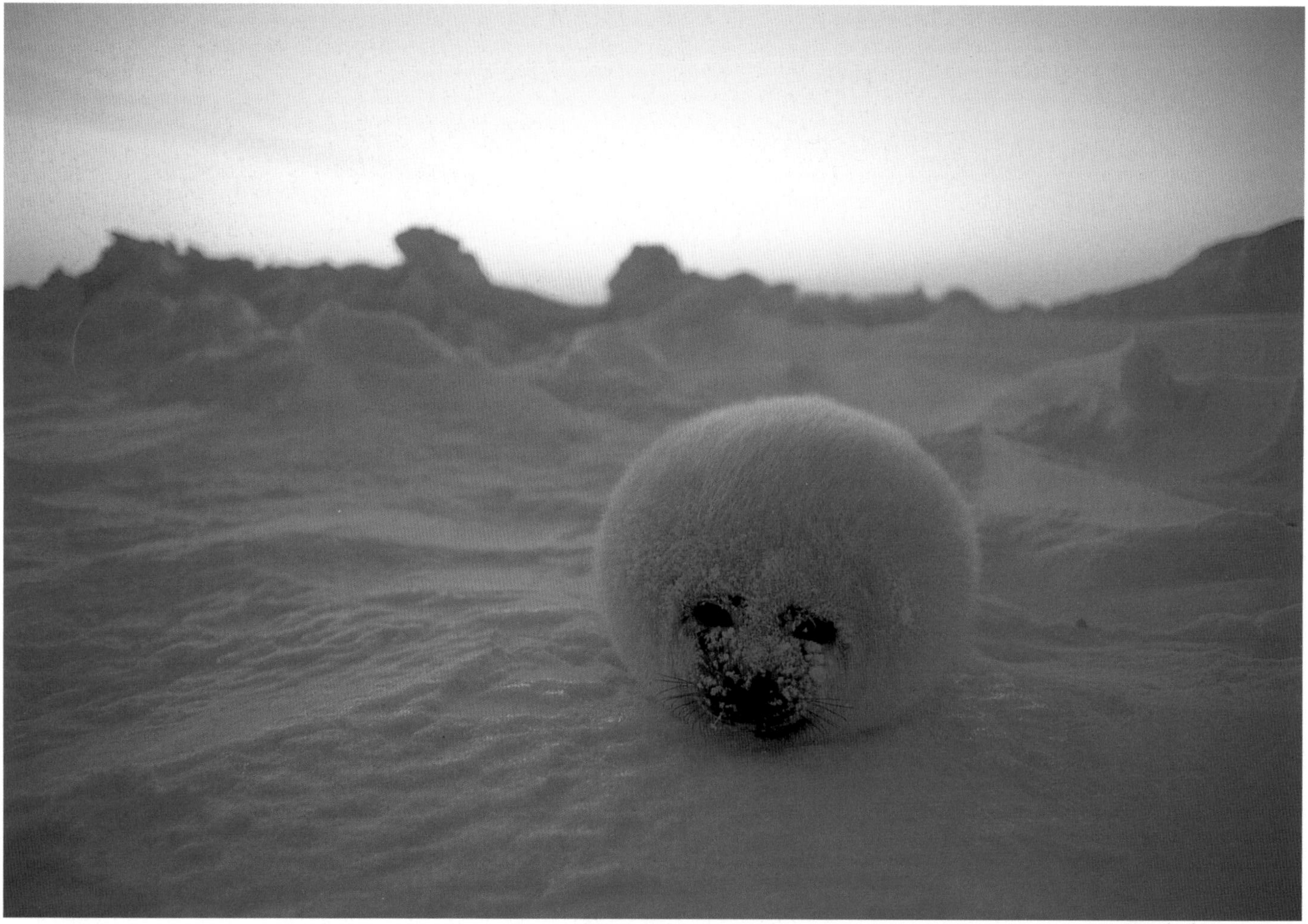

day twelve

After the mother seal is gone, the pup sheds its white fur. It scratches its head and chin with its front flippers, and the white fur floats away. As grey spots appear in its place, the pup gives up crying for its mother and starts playing by itself. Before long, the playful cries fade and the ice plains turn silent. Spring is coming.

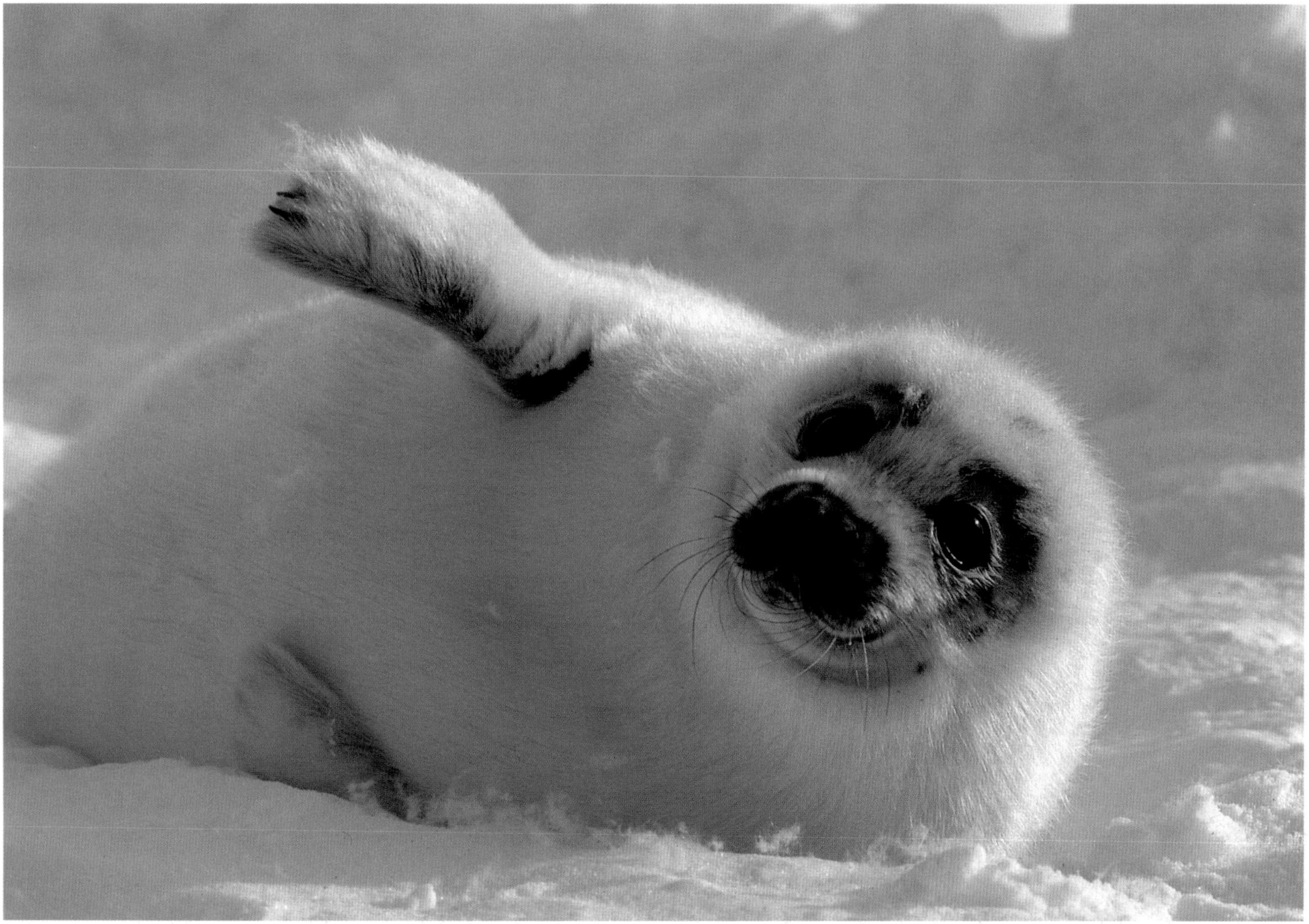

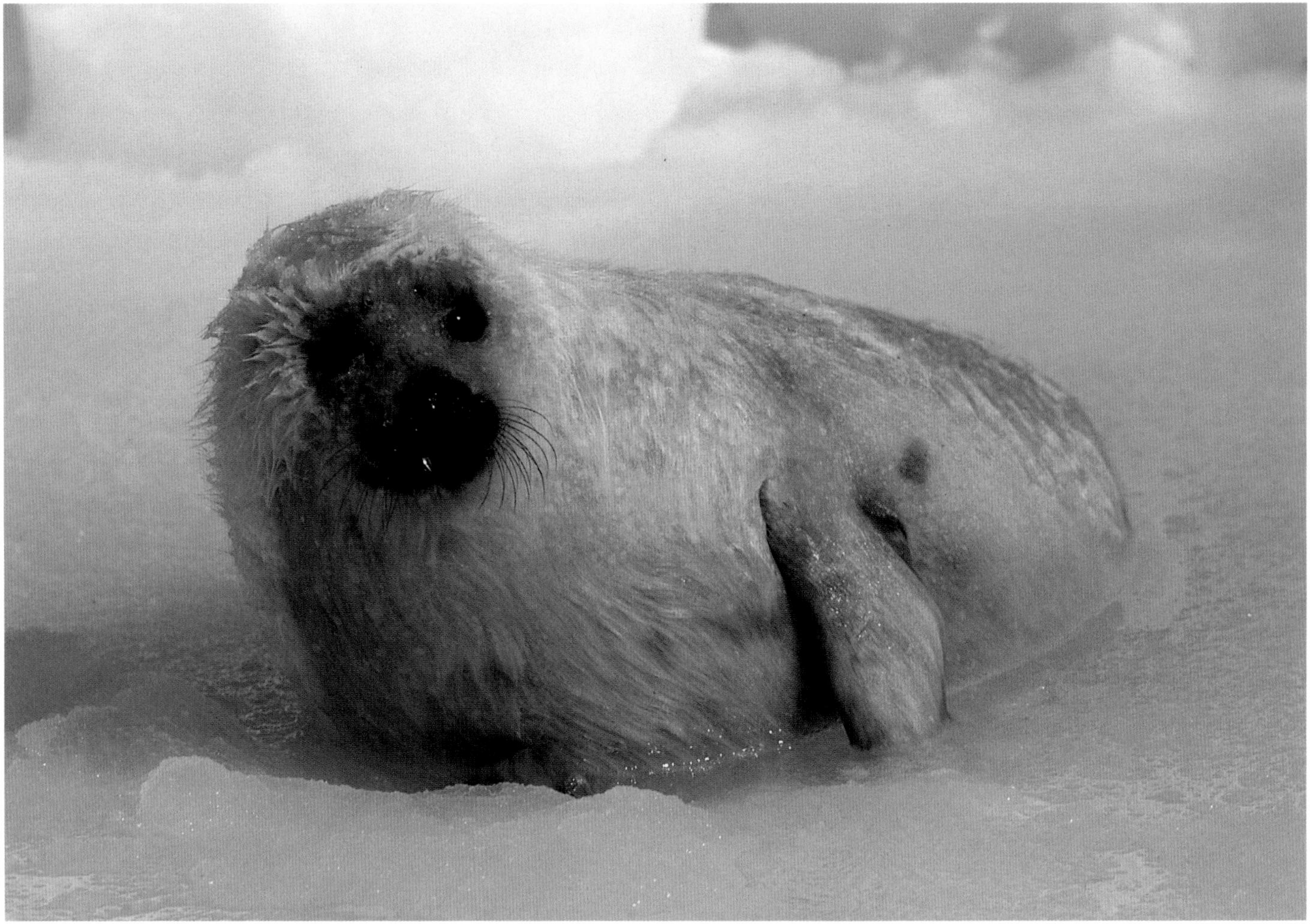

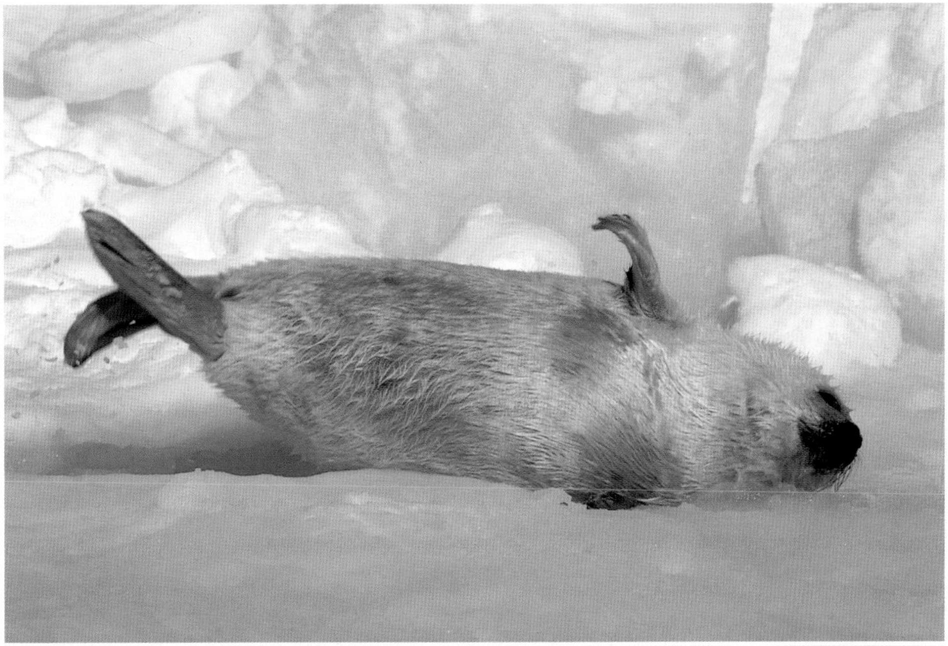

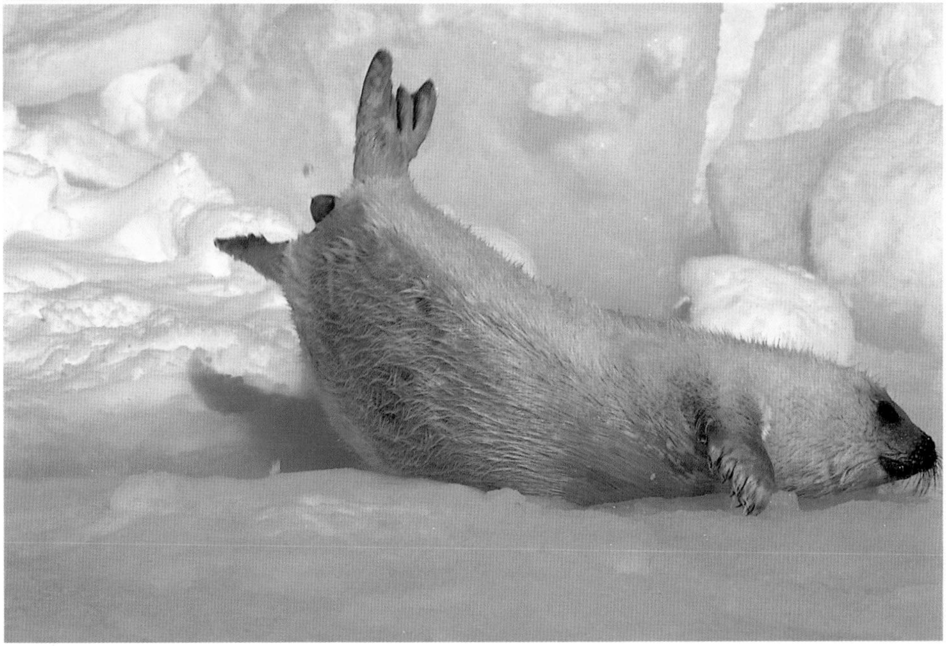

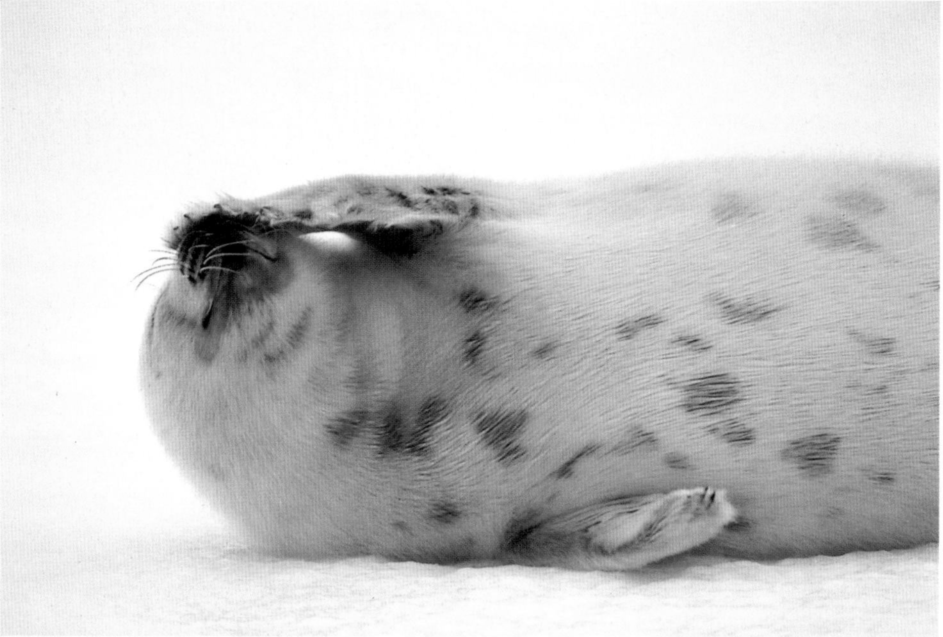
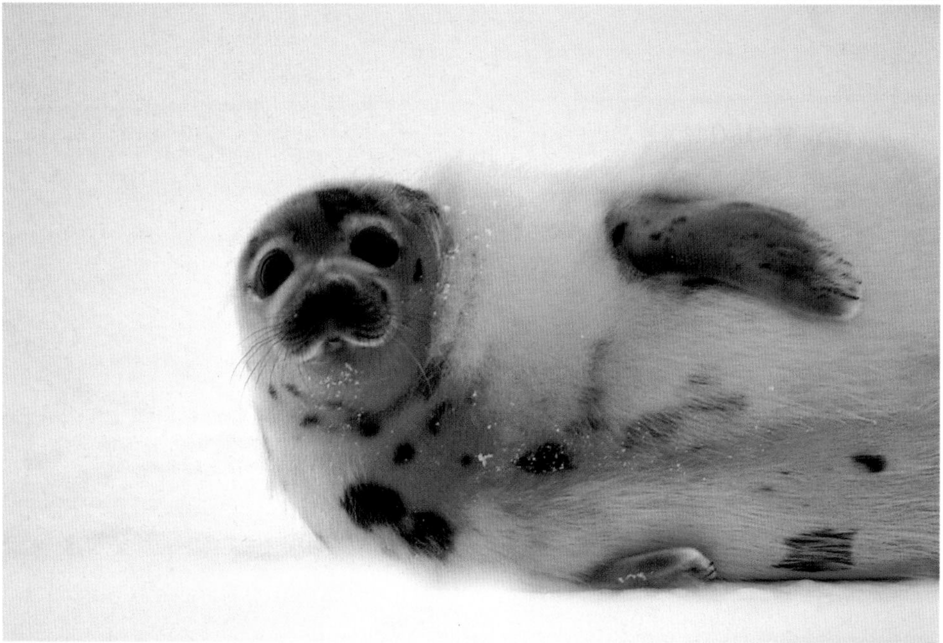

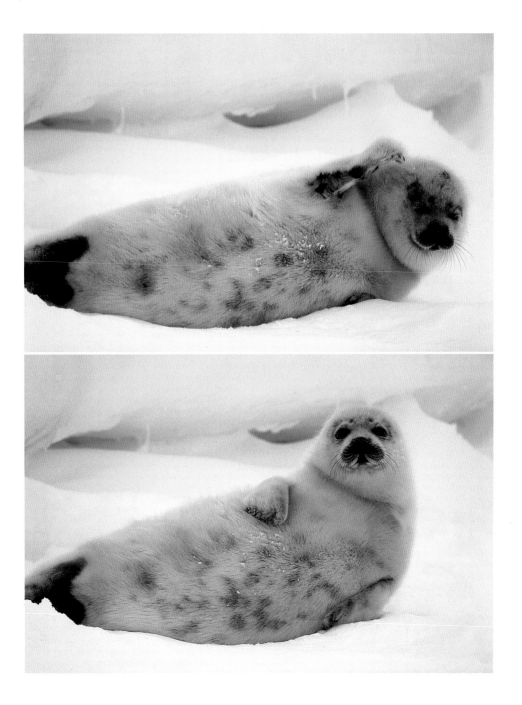

day twenty-two

Is the pup's fur white to camouflage it on the ice plains? Or is it white to keep it warm?
As the color of the fur on the pup's head, neck, and back changes, it forms a unique pattern.

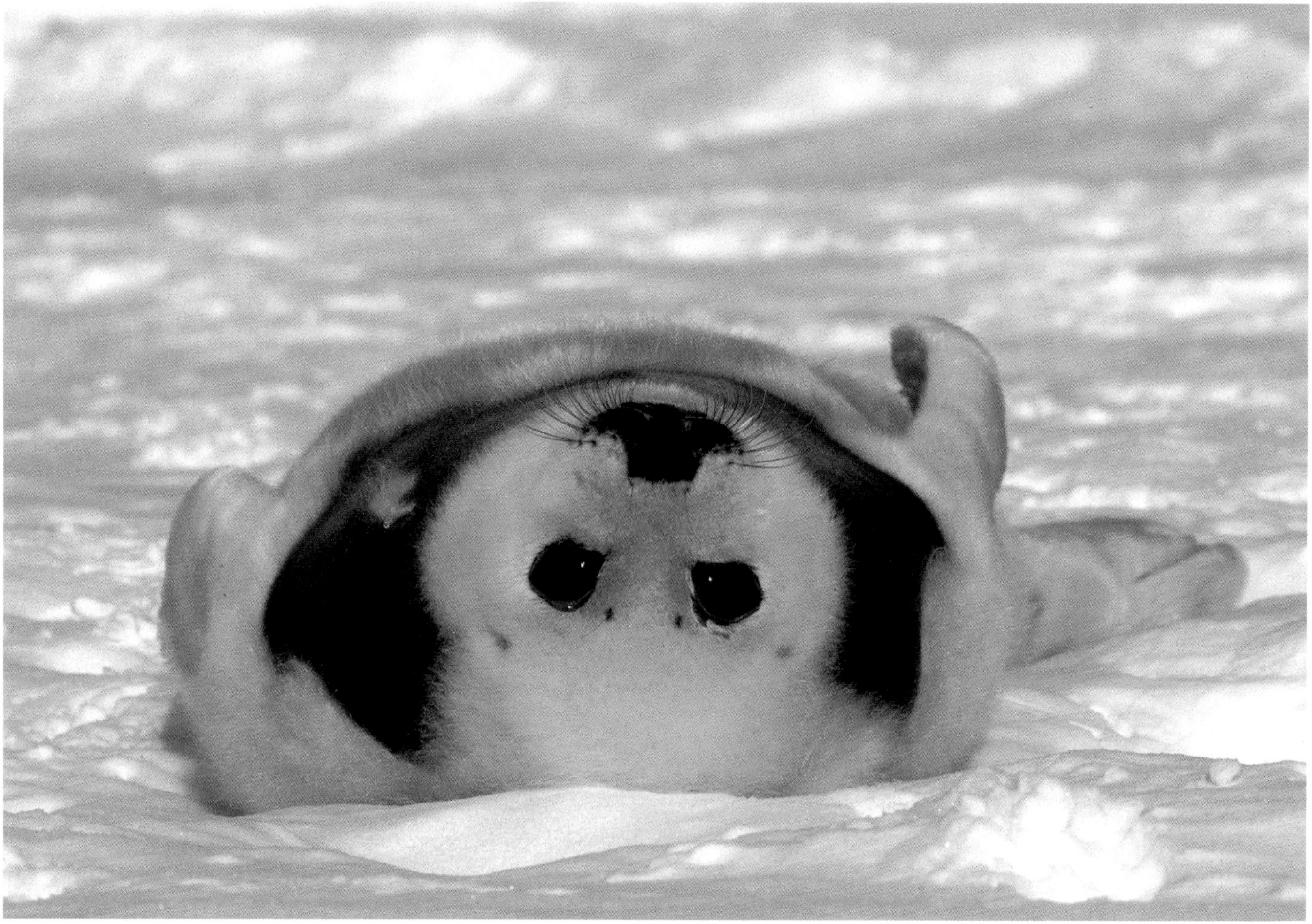

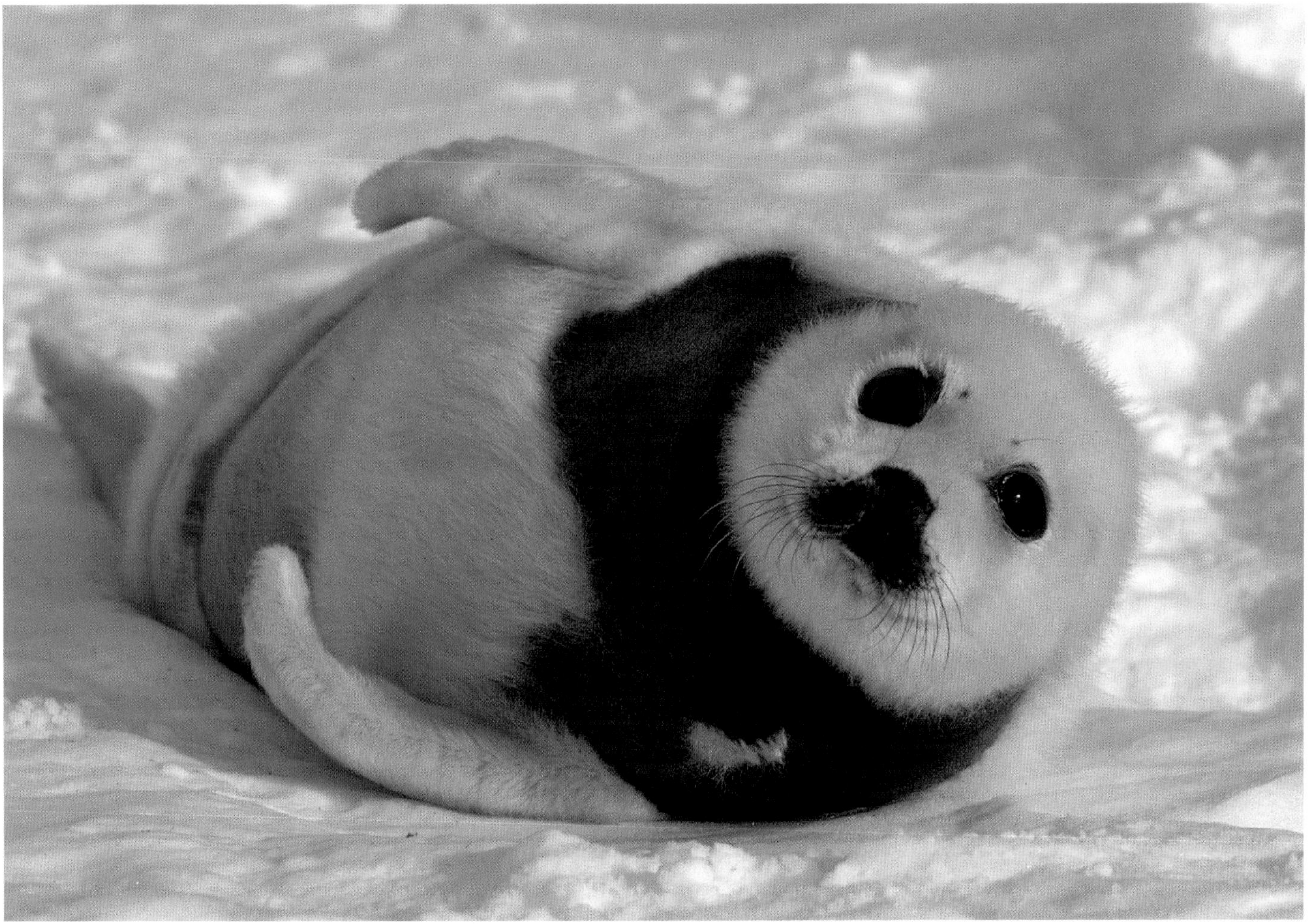

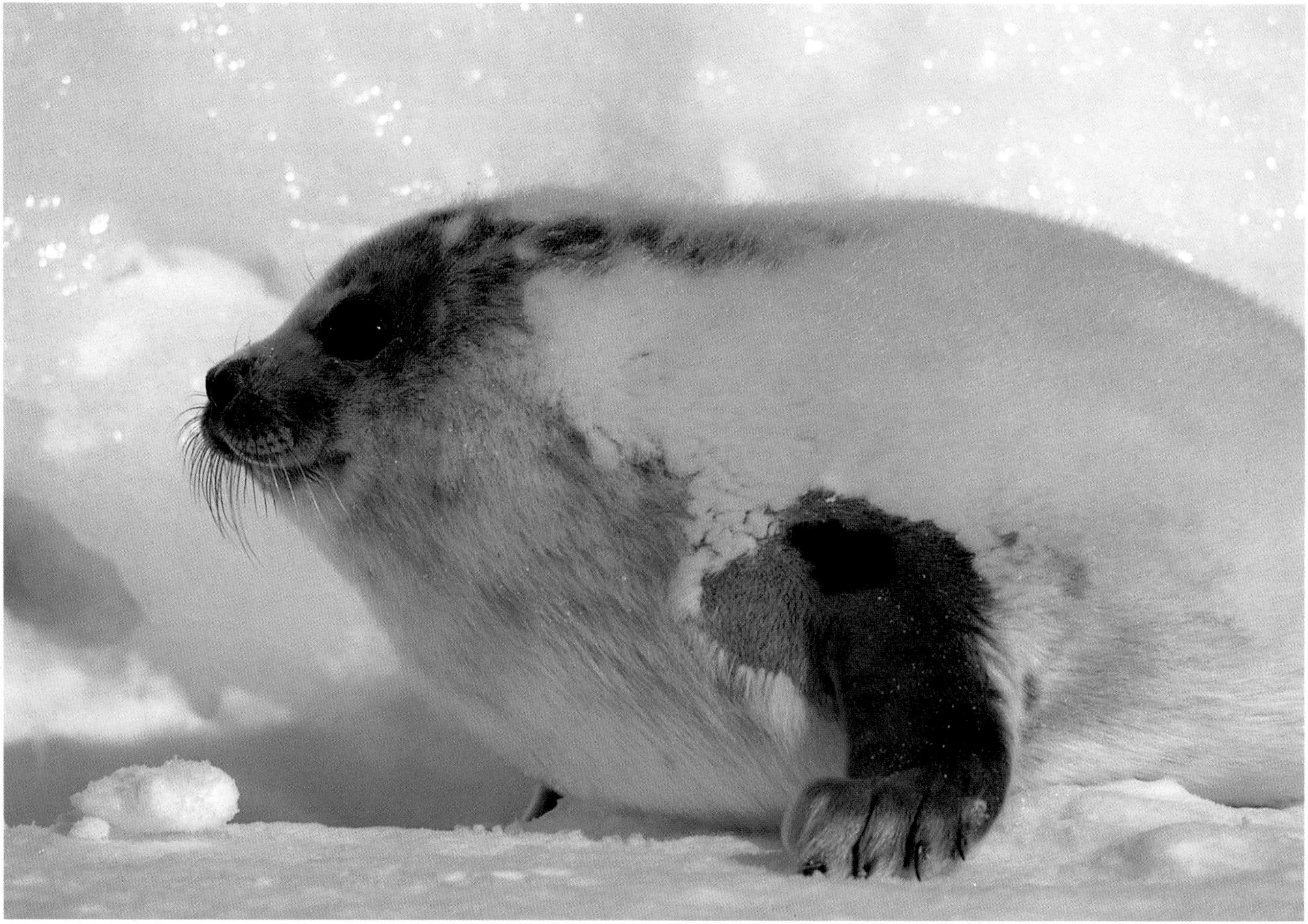

day twenty-six

Once the fur transformation is complete, the pup must become independent. The cracks in the ice spread, giving way to the sea. Water splashes from the flippers of pups practicing their swimming. As they glide along the edge of the ice, the motion of their flippers gradually becomes smoother. At the end of March there is a rich supply of plankton and small fish for them to eat. The famished pups feed for several weeks. Then, one by one, they depart the gulf where they were born and head for the northern seas.

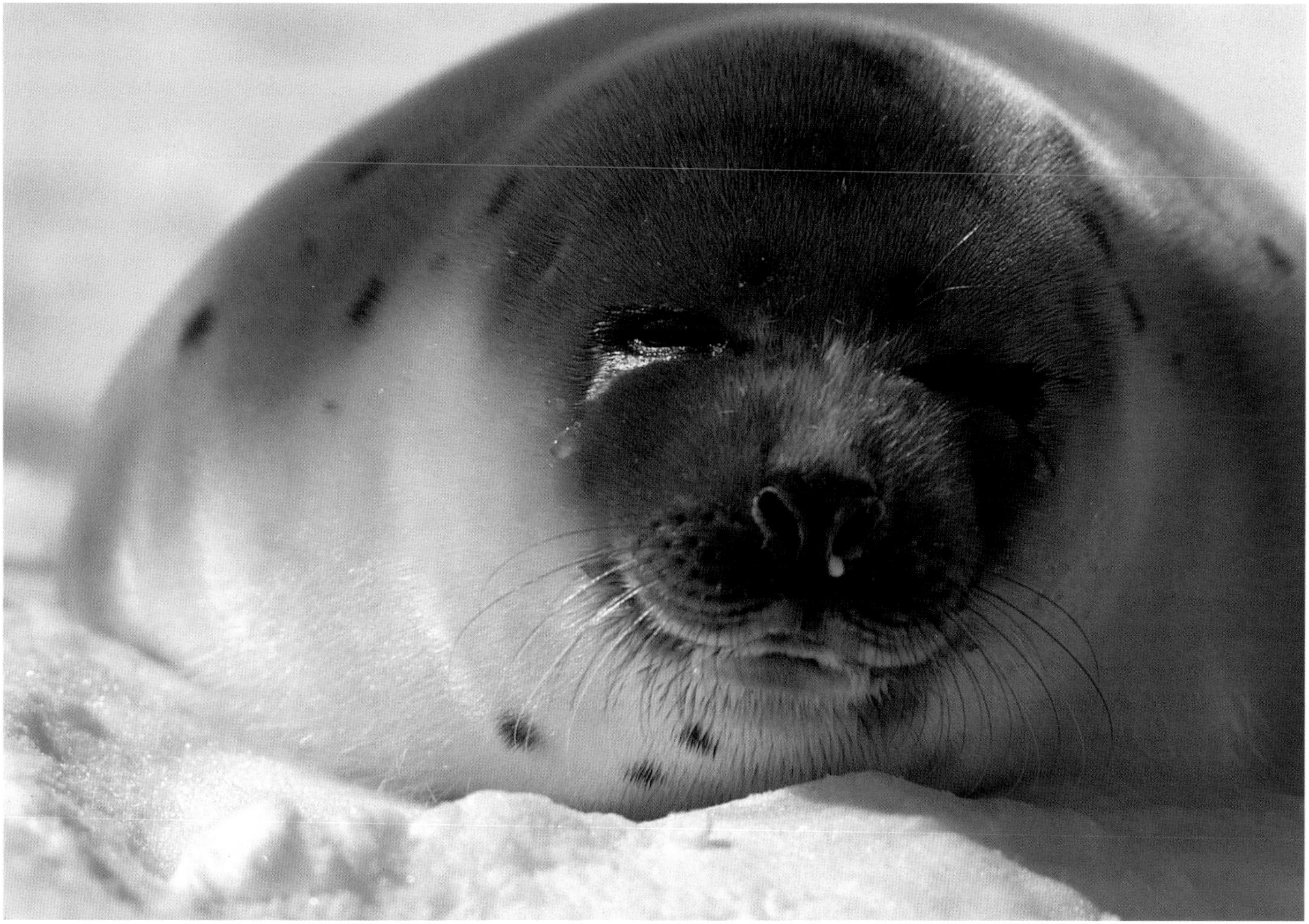

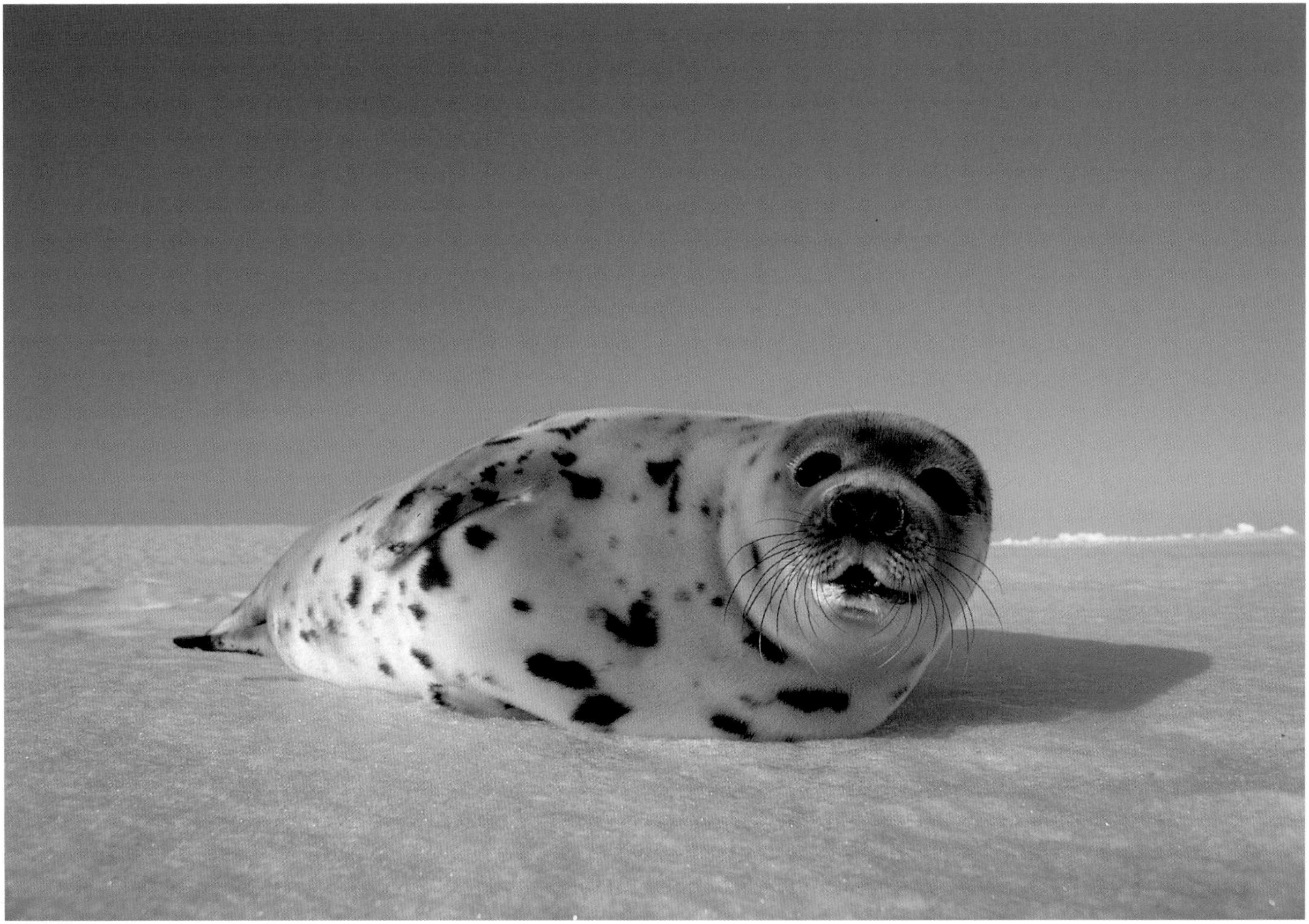

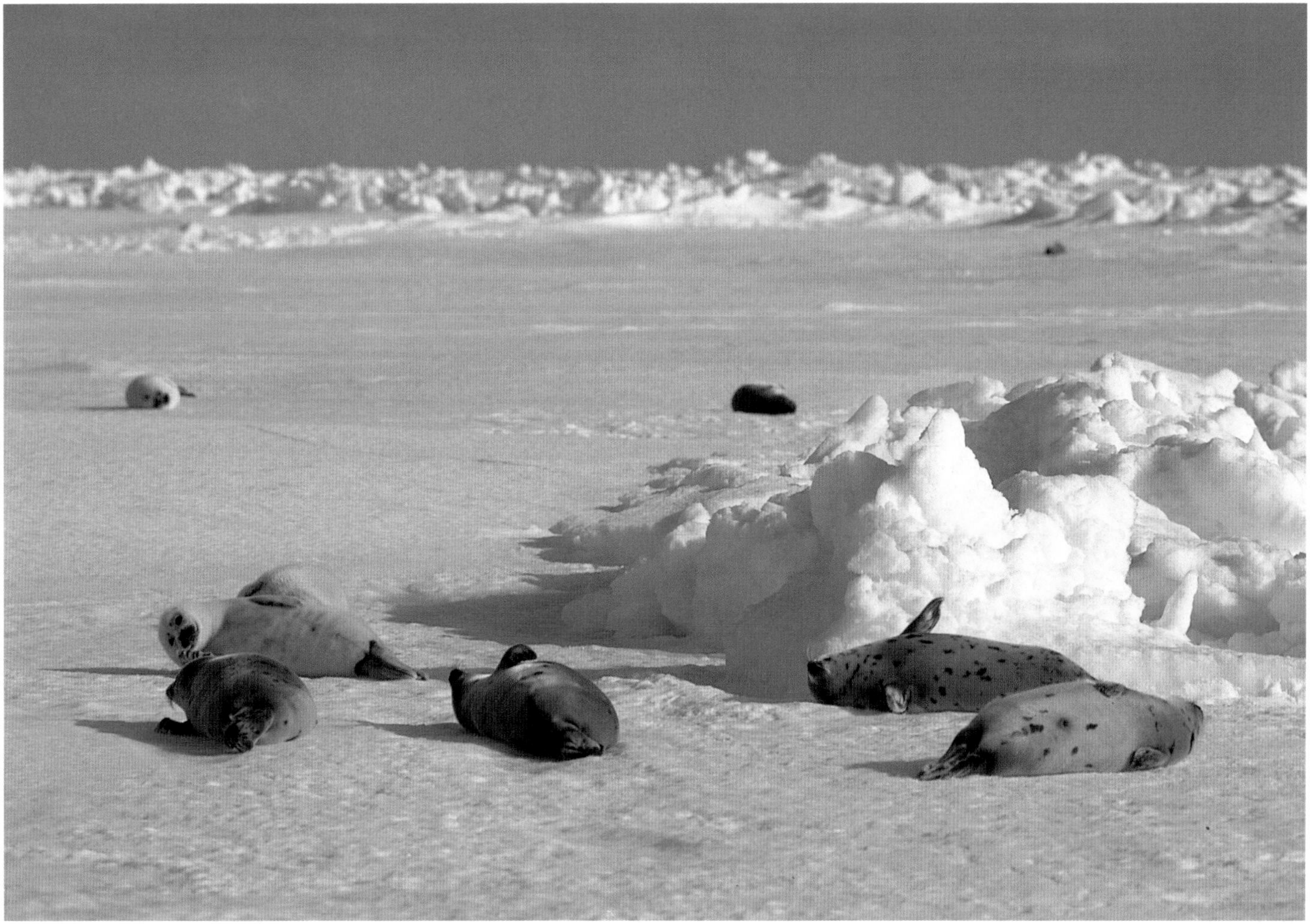

one day

As we flew over the Gulf of Saint Lawrence, off the shores of the Madeleine Islands, I saw seal hunters pulling their boat like a sled, returning from a hunt.

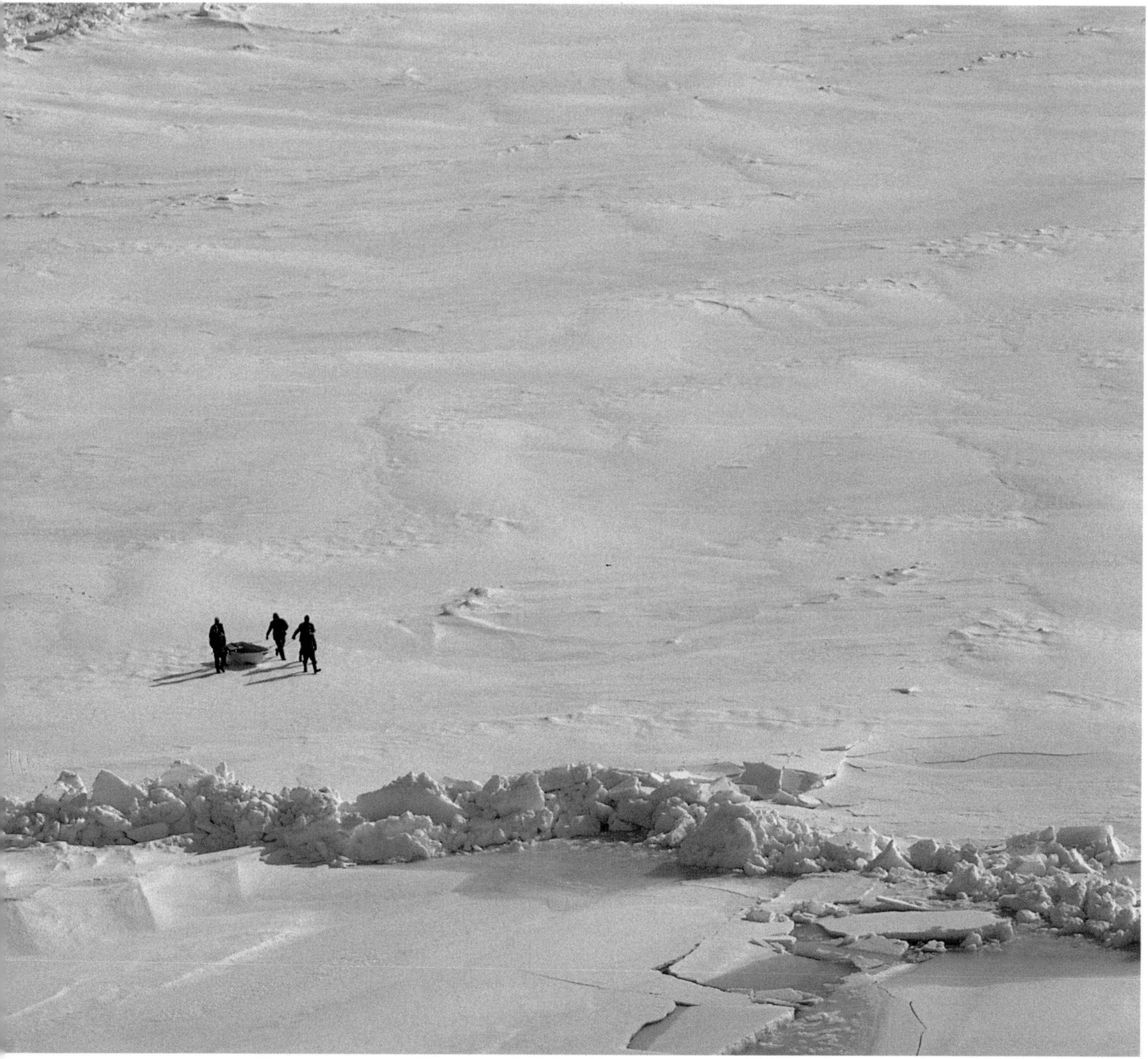

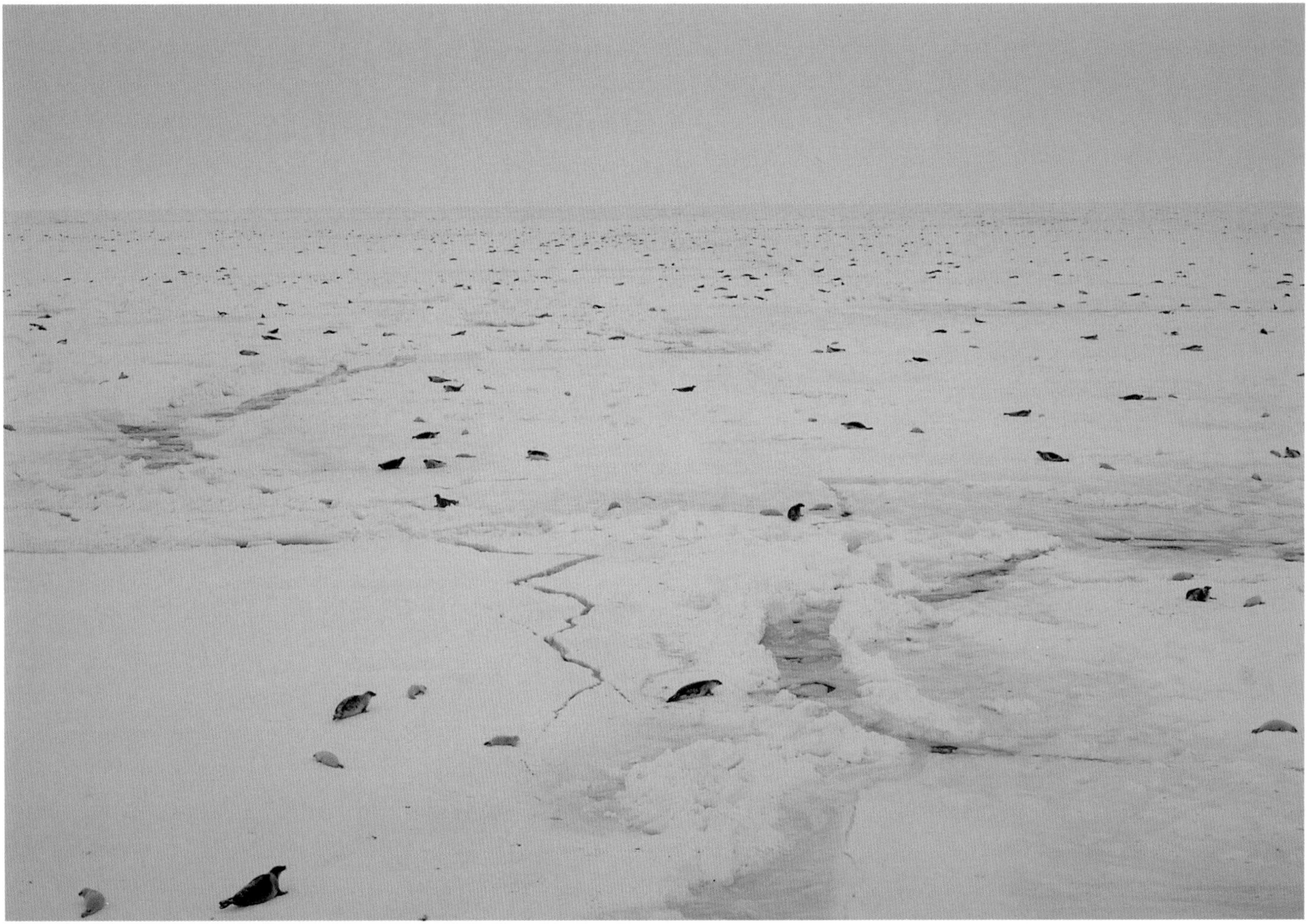

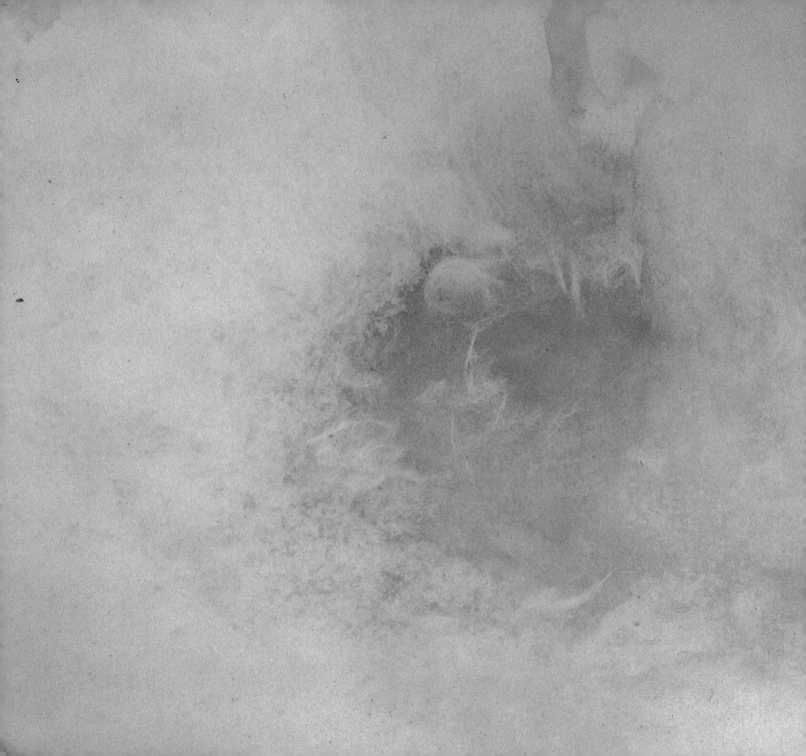